Identity Lifecycle Management

James Relington

DEDICATION

This book is dedicated to all the professionals working tirelessly to secure digital identities and protect organizations from ever-evolving threats. To the cybersecurity teams, IT administrators, and identity management experts who ensure safe and seamless access for users—your work is invaluable. And to my family and friends, whose support and encouragement made this journey possible, thank you.

AKNOWLEDGEMENTS

I would like to express my deepest gratitude to everyone who contributed to the creation of this book. To my colleagues and mentors in the cybersecurity and identity management field, your insights and expertise have been invaluable. To the organizations and professionals who shared their experiences and best practices, your contributions have enriched this work. A special thanks to my family and friends for their unwavering support and encouragement throughout this journey. Finally, to the readers, thank you for your interest in identity lifecycle management—may this book help you navigate the evolving landscape of digital security with confidence.

Introduction to Identity Lifecycle Management

Identity Lifecycle Management (ILM) is a critical component of modern IT and security strategies, ensuring that digital identities are created, maintained, and deactivated in a controlled and secure manner. As organizations expand their digital footprint, managing user identities effectively has become essential for security, compliance, and operational efficiency. Without a structured approach, identity-related risks can lead to data breaches, unauthorized access, and inefficiencies in managing user access across various systems.

At its core, ILM encompasses the entire journey of a user's identity within an organization, from the moment they join to the point they leave or change roles. This process includes provisioning new accounts, managing access rights, handling role changes, and ultimately deactivating accounts when they are no longer needed. Each phase of the identity lifecycle must be carefully managed to minimize security risks and ensure seamless user experiences.

Provisioning is the first step in the identity lifecycle, where a new digital identity is created for an employee, contractor, or partner. This typically involves assigning user credentials, providing access to necessary systems, and ensuring that the individual has the right permissions based on their role. Automation plays a crucial role in this phase, reducing the time required to grant access while minimizing human errors that can lead to security gaps. Without an efficient provisioning process, new employees might experience delays in gaining access to critical resources, impacting productivity.

Once an identity is created, it must be continuously maintained and updated as the user's role or responsibilities change. This is where access management becomes a key aspect of ILM. Organizations must ensure that users only have access to the systems and data they need to perform their job functions. Excessive permissions can lead to security vulnerabilities, while insufficient access can hinder productivity. Regular access reviews and automated adjustments based on job role changes are necessary to maintain the balance between security and efficiency.

One of the major challenges in ILM is handling role changes within an organization. Employees may get promoted, transferred to different departments, or take on additional responsibilities that require new access rights. If these transitions are not managed effectively, users may accumulate excessive privileges over time, leading to what is known as "privilege creep." This can pose significant security risks, as attackers could exploit unnecessary permissions to gain unauthorized access to sensitive information. Implementing a strong Role-Based Access Control (RBAC) or Attribute-Based Access Control (ABAC) model helps in enforcing the principle of least privilege, ensuring that users only have the access they need at any given time.

The final phase of identity lifecycle management is deprovisioning, which involves revoking access when a user leaves the organization or no longer requires certain permissions. Failure to properly deactivate accounts can result in orphaned accounts—user accounts that remain active but are no longer associated with an active employee. These orphaned accounts can be exploited by cybercriminals to gain unauthorized access to corporate systems. Automated deprovisioning ensures that accounts are promptly disabled, reducing the risk of security breaches and ensuring compliance with regulatory requirements.

Security is a fundamental concern throughout the identity lifecycle. Organizations must implement multi-factor authentication (MFA) to enhance security, reducing the risk of unauthorized access due to stolen or compromised credentials. Additionally, continuous monitoring and anomaly detection are essential to identify suspicious activities related to user identities. By leveraging artificial intelligence and machine learning, organizations can detect unusual access patterns and take proactive measures to prevent potential security threats.

Compliance is another driving factor behind effective ILM practices. Many industries are subject to strict regulatory requirements, such as GDPR, HIPAA, and SOX, which mandate proper identity management controls. Organizations must demonstrate that they have effective identity governance processes in place, including regular access audits, policy enforcement, and secure identity management practices. Non-compliance can result in hefty fines and reputational damage, making ILM an essential component of regulatory adherence.

As technology continues to evolve, so does the complexity of managing identities across multiple environments. With the increasing adoption of cloud computing, hybrid infrastructures, and remote workforces, organizations must adapt their ILM strategies to accommodate these changes. Cloud-based identity solutions, federated identity management, and decentralized identity models are emerging as innovative approaches to address modern identity challenges.

Identity Lifecycle Management is not just about security and compliance; it also plays a vital role in improving user experience and operational efficiency. By implementing automated workflows, self-service capabilities, and intelligent access management solutions, organizations can streamline identity processes while reducing administrative overhead. A well-designed ILM strategy not only enhances security but also enables organizations to operate more efficiently in an increasingly digital world.

The Fundamentals of Digital Identity

Digital identity is the foundation of modern online interactions, allowing individuals, organizations, and systems to authenticate, communicate, and transact securely in a digital environment. As technology continues to evolve, the concept of digital identity has become increasingly complex, incorporating various elements such as credentials, authentication methods, and identity attributes. Without a well-defined digital identity framework, securing access to online services, protecting sensitive information, and ensuring compliance with regulatory standards would be nearly impossible.

At its core, digital identity represents the unique characteristics and credentials associated with an individual or entity in the digital world. Unlike physical identity, which is verified through documents such as passports or driver's licenses, digital identity relies on electronic data to establish authenticity. This data may include usernames, passwords, biometric information, cryptographic keys, and other identifiers that link an individual to their online persona. Organizations must implement robust identity management systems to verify and maintain digital identities while safeguarding them from unauthorized access and fraud.

Authentication is a critical component of digital identity, ensuring that a user or entity is who they claim to be. Traditional authentication methods rely on knowledge-based credentials such as passwords, but these are increasingly being replaced or supplemented by more secure methods such as multi-factor authentication (MFA), biometric verification, and hardware security keys. The shift toward passwordless authentication is gaining momentum as organizations seek to enhance security and reduce the risks associated with credential theft. By implementing stronger authentication mechanisms, businesses can improve user trust and reduce the likelihood of identity-related cyber threats.

Beyond authentication, digital identity encompasses identity attributes that define an individual's role, access rights, and entitlements within an organization or online platform. These attributes may include job titles, security clearance levels, email addresses, and other personal or professional details. Effective identity management requires continuous monitoring and updates to ensure that users have the appropriate level of access at all times. Failure to properly manage identity attributes can lead to security vulnerabilities, such as unauthorized access to sensitive information or excessive privileges that increase the risk of data breaches.

One of the most significant challenges in digital identity management is identity verification. Establishing trust in an online identity is essential, especially for industries that handle sensitive transactions, such as banking, healthcare, and government services. Identity proofing techniques, including document verification, facial recognition, and knowledge-based authentication, help verify the legitimacy of a digital identity before granting access to critical systems. As fraudsters become more sophisticated, organizations must adopt advanced verification methods to prevent identity theft and impersonation.

The concept of federated identity has emerged as a solution to streamline digital identity management across multiple platforms. Federated identity allows users to access various services using a single set of credentials, reducing the need for multiple logins and improving user experience. This approach is commonly implemented through Single Sign-On (SSO) solutions, which enable seamless authentication across different applications and domains. By leveraging identity federation, organizations can enhance security while simplifying access management for employees and customers.

Another important aspect of digital identity is the principle of identity sovereignty, which emphasizes an individual's control over their own identity information. Traditional identity models rely on centralized authorities, such as governments or corporations, to issue and manage digital identities. However, decentralized identity frameworks, powered by blockchain technology, are gaining traction as a way to give users greater control over their personal data. In a decentralized identity system, individuals can manage and share their credentials without relying on a central authority, reducing the risk of identity theft and data breaches.

The growing reliance on digital identity has also raised concerns about privacy and data protection. Organizations that collect and store identity-related information must comply with stringent regulations, such as the General Data Protection Regulation (GDPR) and the California Consumer Privacy Act (CCPA). These regulations require businesses to implement strong data protection measures, provide transparency in data collection practices, and give users greater control over their personal information. Failure to comply with these regulations can result in significant legal and financial consequences.

As digital interactions become more prevalent, the need for interoperability in identity management is more important than ever. Users expect seamless access to services across different platforms without the burden of managing multiple identities. Standards such as OpenID Connect, OAuth, and Security Assertion Markup Language (SAML) enable secure identity exchange between organizations and service providers, facilitating a more efficient and user-friendly digital experience. Organizations that adopt these standards can improve security, enhance user convenience, and reduce administrative overhead associated with identity management.

The future of digital identity is evolving rapidly, with emerging technologies such as artificial intelligence, machine learning, and biometrics playing a crucial role in identity verification and fraud detection. AI-driven identity analytics can detect anomalies in user behavior, identify potential security threats, and enhance authentication processes. Biometric authentication methods, including fingerprint scanning, facial recognition, and voice recognition, are becoming more widespread as organizations seek to improve security and convenience. However, these technologies also raise ethical concerns, particularly regarding data privacy, bias in AI algorithms, and the potential for misuse by malicious actors.

A well-implemented digital identity strategy is essential for ensuring security, trust, and efficiency in online interactions. Organizations must continuously adapt to evolving threats, regulatory requirements, and technological advancements to maintain a secure and user-friendly identity management framework. The ability to verify, authenticate, and protect digital identities is fundamental to the success of digital transformation initiatives across industries. As the digital landscape continues to expand, robust identity management practices will remain a cornerstone of cybersecurity and data protection strategies.

Identity and Access Management (IAM) Basics

Identity and Access Management (IAM) is a fundamental discipline in cybersecurity that focuses on ensuring the right individuals have access to the right resources at the right times and for the right reasons. As organizations expand their digital infrastructure, managing user identities and controlling access to critical systems and data has become an essential component of security, efficiency, and compliance. Without a well-structured IAM framework, organizations face increased risks of data breaches, insider threats, and operational inefficiencies that can lead to financial and reputational damage.

At its core, IAM encompasses the processes, policies, and technologies used to manage digital identities and their access privileges within an organization. It provides mechanisms for authentication, authorization, and identity governance to enforce security policies while enabling seamless user experiences. A well-implemented IAM system helps organizations streamline access management, reduce the complexity of handling multiple credentials, and protect sensitive data from unauthorized access.

Authentication is one of the primary components of IAM, ensuring that users, devices, and applications are who they claim to be before granting access to systems or information. Traditionally, authentication has relied on usernames and passwords, but as cyber threats have evolved, organizations have moved toward more secure authentication methods. Multi-factor authentication (MFA) has become a standard security measure, requiring users to provide multiple pieces of evidence, such as a password, a fingerprint, or a security token, to verify their identity. By implementing stronger authentication mechanisms, organizations can mitigate the risks associated with stolen credentials and unauthorized access.

Beyond authentication, IAM also focuses on authorization, which determines the level of access granted to authenticated users. Authorization ensures that users can only access the resources necessary for their role within an organization. Role-Based Access Control (RBAC) is a widely used approach to managing authorization, where users are assigned roles based on their job functions, and each role has predefined access rights. This method helps enforce the principle of least privilege, reducing the risk of excessive permissions that could be exploited by attackers or misused by employees. Another approach, Attribute-Based Access Control (ABAC), evaluates user attributes such as department, location, or security clearance to determine access rights dynamically.

Identity governance plays a critical role in IAM by providing oversight and accountability for identity-related activities. Organizations must regularly review and audit user access to ensure compliance with security policies and regulatory requirements. Identity governance solutions enable businesses to automate access reviews, detect policy violations, and enforce segregation of duties to prevent conflicts of interest. Without proper identity governance, organizations may struggle to maintain visibility into who has access to what resources, leading to security gaps and compliance risks.

The concept of identity lifecycle management is closely linked to IAM, covering the entire journey of a user's identity from creation to deactivation. When a new employee joins an organization, IAM systems facilitate user provisioning by automatically creating accounts, assigning roles, and granting access to necessary applications. As employees change roles or responsibilities, IAM ensures that access rights are adjusted accordingly, preventing unnecessary accumulation of privileges. When an employee leaves the organization, deprovisioning processes revoke all access rights to eliminate the risk of orphaned accounts that could be exploited by cybercriminals.

IAM solutions also extend beyond traditional corporate networks to cloud environments, third-party vendors, and external partners. The adoption of cloud computing and remote work has introduced new challenges in identity management, requiring organizations to implement federated identity and Single Sign-On (SSO) solutions. Federated identity allows users to authenticate across multiple systems and organizations using a single set of credentials, reducing the need for redundant logins and improving user convenience. SSO simplifies access management by enabling users to log in once and gain access to multiple applications without re-entering credentials.

The increasing complexity of IT environments has led to the rise of Identity-as-a-Service (IDaaS), a cloud-based approach to IAM that provides scalable identity management solutions. IDaaS platforms offer centralized identity administration, strong authentication mechanisms, and integration with cloud applications, reducing the burden on internal IT teams. Organizations leveraging IDaaS can enhance security while ensuring seamless access for employees, contractors, and customers across different digital platforms.

IAM is also a key component of cybersecurity frameworks such as Zero Trust, which assumes that no user or device should be inherently trusted, even within the corporate network. Zero Trust IAM enforces strict identity verification, continuous authentication, and adaptive access controls based on real-time risk assessments. By implementing

Zero Trust principles, organizations can minimize the attack surface and protect sensitive data from both external and internal threats.

Regulatory compliance is another driving force behind IAM adoption, as many industries must adhere to strict security and privacy regulations. Frameworks such as GDPR, HIPAA, and NIST require organizations to implement robust identity management controls, conduct regular access audits, and protect user data from unauthorized exposure. Non-compliance can result in severe penalties, making IAM an essential component of risk management and regulatory adherence.

As the digital landscape continues to evolve, IAM will remain a critical pillar of cybersecurity, ensuring secure access to applications, systems, and data. Organizations must continuously refine their IAM strategies, adopt emerging identity technologies, and enforce strong security policies to protect against identity-related threats. By leveraging automation, artificial intelligence, and advanced authentication mechanisms, businesses can enhance their security posture while providing seamless and secure access experiences for their users.

User Provisioning and Deprovisioning

User provisioning and deprovisioning are essential processes in identity lifecycle management, ensuring that employees, contractors, and third-party users receive the appropriate access to systems and applications when they join an organization and that their access is promptly revoked when they leave. These processes are fundamental to maintaining security, compliance, and operational efficiency in an increasingly complex IT environment. Without proper provisioning and deprovisioning mechanisms, organizations risk unauthorized access, security breaches, and inefficiencies that can disrupt business operations.

User provisioning is the process of creating and managing user accounts, assigning roles, and granting access to necessary resources based on job functions. When a new employee is hired, their digital identity must be established, allowing them to access email, enterprise applications, databases, and collaboration tools. Traditionally, provisioning was a manual task, requiring IT administrators to create accounts and assign permissions individually. However, manual provisioning is time-consuming and prone to human error, leading to inconsistencies in access levels and security vulnerabilities.

Automated provisioning has become the standard approach, leveraging identity and access management (IAM) solutions to streamline account creation and role assignments. By integrating IAM systems with human resources (HR) platforms, organizations can synchronize user identities and automatically grant access based on predefined rules. This ensures that new employees receive the necessary permissions on their first day, eliminating delays and improving productivity. Additionally, automation reduces the risk of misconfigurations, ensuring that users do not receive excessive privileges that could expose sensitive data to unauthorized access.

Role-based access control (RBAC) is commonly used in provisioning to assign permissions based on job functions. Employees in similar roles receive the same level of access, ensuring consistency across the organization. In more dynamic environments, attribute-based access control (ABAC) can be implemented, allowing access decisions to be made based on user attributes such as department, location, or security clearance. Both RBAC and ABAC help organizations enforce the principle of least privilege, ensuring that users have only the access necessary to perform their job functions.

As employees progress within an organization, their roles and responsibilities often change. Promotions, department transfers, or temporary assignments may require modifications to their access rights. Failure to properly adjust permissions can lead to privilege creep, where users accumulate excessive access over time. This poses a significant security risk, as attackers can exploit unnecessary privileges to gain unauthorized control over critical systems. Regular access reviews and automated entitlement management help prevent privilege creep by ensuring that access rights are continuously updated to reflect job changes.

While provisioning ensures that employees can perform their duties effectively, deprovisioning is equally critical in protecting an organization's data and systems. When an employee resigns, is terminated, or no longer requires certain access rights, their accounts and permissions must be promptly revoked. Delays in deprovisioning can result in orphaned accounts—active accounts that are no longer associated with a valid user. These accounts pose a serious security risk, as attackers can exploit them to gain unauthorized access without detection.

Automated deprovisioning ensures that access is revoked in real time, reducing the risk of security breaches. By integrating IAM solutions with HR and directory services, organizations can trigger automatic account deactivation when an employee's status changes in the HR system. This approach eliminates the reliance on manual intervention, preventing oversight and ensuring compliance with security policies. Additionally, automated workflows can notify relevant stakeholders, such as managers and security teams, to verify that all necessary access revocations have been completed.

In some cases, organizations implement phased deprovisioning, where access is gradually revoked based on predefined policies. For example, an employee leaving a company may first lose access to non-essential systems while retaining email and HR system access for a limited period. This approach allows for a smoother transition, ensuring that departing employees can complete exit procedures while minimizing security risks. However, phased deprovisioning must be carefully managed to prevent unauthorized access to sensitive information.

Deprovisioning is not limited to employee departures; it also applies to temporary access and third-party users. Contractors, vendors, and external partners often require access to enterprise systems for a limited time. Without proper governance, these users may retain access long after their engagement ends, creating an unnecessary security risk. Implementing time-based access policies and automatic expiration for temporary accounts helps mitigate this risk by ensuring that access is revoked when it is no longer needed.

Audit and compliance requirements also play a significant role in the provisioning and deprovisioning processes. Regulations such as GDPR, HIPAA, and SOX mandate strict controls over user access to protect sensitive data and ensure accountability. Organizations must maintain detailed records of user access changes, including who was granted access, when modifications were made, and who approved the changes. Regular audits help identify discrepancies and enforce security policies, reducing the risk of non-compliance and potential legal consequences.

Organizations that fail to implement effective provisioning and deprovisioning strategies often experience inefficiencies, increased security risks, and compliance challenges. Users may experience delays in obtaining access to critical resources, leading to decreased productivity and frustration. On the other hand, excessive access rights can result in insider threats, where employees or attackers exploit privileged accounts to steal data or disrupt operations. By leveraging IAM automation, access control frameworks, and continuous monitoring, businesses can ensure that user accounts are managed securely throughout the entire identity lifecycle.

As organizations continue to adopt cloud-based applications, hybrid IT environments, and remote work policies, the complexity of user provisioning and deprovisioning will increase. IAM solutions must evolve to support dynamic access management, adaptive authentication, and identity analytics to detect and respond to anomalous access behaviors. Implementing a robust provisioning and deprovisioning strategy is not only a security necessity but also a key factor in enabling digital transformation and maintaining trust in the enterprise's identity management practices.

Role-Based Access Control (RBAC)

Role-Based Access Control (RBAC) is a widely used approach to managing user access within an organization, ensuring that users have the permissions necessary to perform their job functions while minimizing security risks associated with excessive or unauthorized access. By assigning permissions based on roles rather than individual users, RBAC simplifies access management, enhances security, and improves operational efficiency. As organizations grow and their IT environments become more complex, RBAC provides a scalable and structured method to manage access across multiple systems, applications, and data repositories.

At its core, RBAC operates on the principle of least privilege, which dictates that users should only be granted the minimum level of access required to perform their duties. This principle reduces the risk of security breaches by limiting the potential damage an attacker could cause if a user's account is compromised. By grouping permissions into roles that reflect specific job functions, organizations can ensure that users have appropriate access without the need to manually assign and track individual permissions for each user. For example, a role for a financial analyst may include access to accounting software and financial reports, while a marketing specialist's role may grant access to customer relationship management (CRM) tools and marketing analytics.

The implementation of RBAC begins with defining roles and their associated permissions. Roles are typically designed to align with organizational structures, job responsibilities, and business processes. It is essential to conduct a thorough analysis of the organization's operations to identify the access requirements for each role. This process involves collaborating with department heads, IT teams, and compliance officers to ensure that roles accurately reflect business needs and security policies. Poorly defined roles can lead to over-provisioning or under-provisioning of access, resulting in security risks and operational inefficiencies.

Once roles are established, users are assigned to roles based on their job functions. When a user is added to a role, they inherit all the permissions associated with that role. This inheritance mechanism simplifies access management by allowing administrators to manage permissions at the role level rather than individually for each user. When a user's job responsibilities change, their access can be easily updated by reassigning them to a different role. This streamlined approach not only reduces administrative overhead but also ensures that access rights are consistent and up to date.

One of the key advantages of RBAC is its ability to enforce separation of duties (SoD), a critical security concept that prevents conflicts of interest and reduces the risk of fraud. By defining roles that separate critical tasks, such as approving financial transactions and processing payments, organizations can ensure that no single individual has the ability to perform conflicting actions. SoD policies are particularly important in industries such as finance, healthcare, and government, where regulatory compliance and accountability are paramount. RBAC makes it easier to implement and enforce SoD by structuring roles in a way that aligns with these policies.

RBAC also enhances security by making it easier to revoke access when it is no longer needed. When an employee leaves the organization or changes roles, their access can be quickly modified or revoked by updating their role assignments. This reduces the risk of orphaned accounts and privilege creep, where users accumulate excessive permissions over time. Automated identity and access management (IAM) solutions further improve this process by integrating with human resources systems to trigger role changes and access revocations based on employment status updates.

While RBAC offers numerous benefits, its effectiveness depends on proper role design and ongoing maintenance. Organizations must regularly review and update roles to reflect changes in business processes, organizational structure, and security requirements. Over time, roles may become outdated or redundant, leading to inefficiencies and security gaps. Role mining, a process of analyzing user access patterns to identify optimal role structures, can help organizations refine their RBAC implementations and ensure that roles remain relevant and efficient.

RBAC is not a one-size-fits-all solution, and its implementation can vary based on an organization's size, complexity, and industry. In large enterprises with diverse job functions and complex access requirements, a hierarchical RBAC model may be used. This model introduces role hierarchies, where higher-level roles inherit the permissions of lower-level roles. For example, a manager role may inherit the permissions of a staff role while also having additional privileges related to supervisory tasks. Hierarchical RBAC simplifies access management by reducing the number of roles and allowing for more efficient permission assignment.

In dynamic environments where access requirements are constantly changing, RBAC can be combined with attribute-based access control (ABAC) to provide more granular and flexible access decisions. While RBAC relies on static role assignments, ABAC evaluates user attributes, such as location, device type, and security clearance, to determine access rights in real time. This hybrid approach allows organizations to maintain the simplicity and scalability of RBAC while addressing complex and context-specific access needs.

Compliance and auditability are additional benefits of RBAC, as it provides a clear and transparent framework for managing and tracking user access. Organizations can generate reports that show which users have access to specific resources, when access was granted, and who approved the access. This level of visibility is essential for demonstrating compliance with regulations such as GDPR, HIPAA, and SOX, which require organizations to maintain strict controls over user access to sensitive data. RBAC simplifies the audit process by providing a centralized and consistent view of access rights across the organization.

As organizations continue to adopt cloud-based services, remote work models, and digital transformation initiatives, the importance of effective access management has never been greater. RBAC remains a cornerstone of identity and access management strategies, providing a structured and scalable approach to controlling access in complex IT environments. By ensuring that users have the right access at the right time and for the right reasons, RBAC helps organizations protect their data, maintain regulatory compliance, and operate efficiently in an ever-changing digital landscape.

Attribute-Based Access Control (ABAC)

Attribute-Based Access Control (ABAC) is an advanced access control model that determines permissions based on attributes associated with users, resources, and environmental conditions. Unlike Role-Based Access Control (RBAC), which assigns access based on predefined roles, ABAC dynamically evaluates attributes in real-time to enforce security policies. This flexibility allows organizations to implement fine-grained access controls, ensuring that users only access the data and applications appropriate for their specific context. As digital environments become more complex, ABAC has emerged as a powerful solution for managing access in dynamic and highly regulated industries.

At the core of ABAC is the concept of attributes, which define characteristics of users, resources, and environmental factors. User attributes may include job title, department, security clearance, location, and authentication method. Resource attributes describe properties of the data or application being accessed, such as classification level, file type, or ownership. Environmental attributes consider factors like time of access, device type, network location, or geographic region. By evaluating a combination of these attributes, organizations can create access policies that are more adaptable than traditional role-based models.

A key advantage of ABAC is its ability to enforce the principle of least privilege dynamically. Instead of assigning static permissions to roles, ABAC evaluates contextual information at the moment of access, ensuring that users receive only the permissions necessary for a specific action. For example, a financial analyst may be allowed to access a financial report only during business hours from a corporate network, but access may be restricted if they attempt to log in from an untrusted location or outside of approved working hours. This contextual enforcement significantly reduces the risk of unauthorized access while maintaining business efficiency.

The implementation of ABAC involves defining access control policies that specify how attributes influence access decisions. These policies follow an "if-then" logic, where conditions determine whether access is granted or denied. For instance, an organization may define a policy stating, "If a user's department is Finance, and the resource classification is Confidential, and the access request occurs from a corporate-issued device, then allow access." By combining multiple attributes, ABAC policies enable organizations to enforce more precise security controls without the limitations of rigid role structures.

Organizations that operate in highly regulated environments benefit significantly from ABAC due to its ability to enforce compliance requirements. Regulations such as GDPR, HIPAA, and NIST mandate strict access controls to protect sensitive data, and ABAC provides the necessary flexibility to enforce these rules without constant manual intervention. For example, healthcare organizations can use ABAC to restrict patient data access based on a doctor's specialty, patient consent status, or treatment location. This ensures that sensitive medical records are accessible only to authorized personnel under specific conditions.

ABAC is particularly well-suited for cloud environments and modern IT infrastructures, where users access resources from various devices and locations. Traditional access control models struggle to handle the complexity of hybrid and multi-cloud environments, but ABAC dynamically adjusts permissions based on contextual factors. A user may be permitted to access a cloud storage system from a managed laptop within the corporate network but denied access if they attempt to log in from a personal smartphone outside of approved regions. This level of granularity enhances security while accommodating the flexibility required in modern work environments.

The adoption of ABAC requires organizations to integrate attribute-based decision-making into their identity and access management (IAM) systems. This involves collecting, managing, and validating attributes from various sources, such as human resources databases, authentication systems, and network monitoring tools. Ensuring the accuracy and integrity of attribute data is critical, as outdated or incorrect attributes can lead to unintended access decisions. Automating attribute updates through identity governance solutions helps maintain a consistent and reliable access control framework.

One of the challenges in implementing ABAC is the complexity of defining and managing policies. Unlike RBAC, where permissions are assigned based on a limited number of roles, ABAC policies can involve multiple attributes and conditions, leading to increased administrative overhead. To address this challenge, organizations must establish clear governance practices, conduct policy reviews, and leverage policy management tools that simplify the creation and enforcement of access rules. Developing a structured policy framework ensures that access decisions remain transparent, auditable, and aligned with business requirements.

Integrating ABAC with existing security technologies enhances its effectiveness and expands its use cases. Combining ABAC with multi-factor authentication (MFA) allows organizations to enforce conditional access based on risk factors. For instance, a high-risk access request from an unusual location may trigger additional authentication steps before granting access. Similarly, integrating ABAC with artificial intelligence (AI) and machine learning enables real-time risk assessment and anomaly detection, further strengthening an organization's security posture.

As cybersecurity threats continue to evolve, ABAC provides a proactive approach to access management that adapts to changing risk conditions. Organizations facing insider threats, privilege escalation attacks, and data exfiltration attempts can leverage ABAC to enforce strict access controls based on real-time evaluations. By continuously assessing user behavior, device health, and network security posture, ABAC helps prevent unauthorized access and data breaches before they occur.

The increasing demand for flexible and scalable access control solutions has positioned ABAC as a preferred model for enterprises undergoing digital transformation. As organizations embrace remote work, cloud computing, and interconnected systems, the ability to dynamically grant and revoke access based on contextual factors becomes essential. ABAC not only enhances security but also improves operational efficiency by reducing the need for manual access adjustments and role-based exceptions. By implementing a robust attribute-based access control strategy, organizations can achieve a balance between security, compliance, and user productivity in an increasingly complex IT landscape.

Identity Governance and Administration (IGA)

Identity Governance and Administration (IGA) is a critical component of identity and access management (IAM), ensuring that organizations maintain visibility, control, and compliance over user identities and their associated access rights. As businesses expand their digital presence, the complexity of managing identities across multiple systems, applications, and environments has increased. IGA provides a structured approach to managing user accounts, enforcing security policies, and ensuring compliance with regulatory requirements, all while minimizing the risks associated with unauthorized access and privilege misuse.

At the heart of IGA is the ability to define, manage, and enforce identity-related policies that govern how users gain and maintain access to enterprise resources. Organizations must ensure that employees, contractors, and third-party users have the appropriate level of access based on their job functions, responsibilities, and security requirements. Without proper governance, organizations risk accumulating excessive permissions, orphaned accounts, and compliance violations that could lead to security breaches or regulatory penalties.

IGA solutions integrate identity lifecycle management with governance capabilities, enabling organizations to automate user provisioning, access reviews, and policy enforcement. User provisioning is a key function within IGA, ensuring that new employees receive the right level of access from their first day on the job. By integrating with human resources (HR) systems, IGA platforms can automatically create accounts, assign roles, and grant permissions based on predefined policies. This automation reduces administrative overhead while ensuring consistency in access control. Similarly, when employees change roles or leave the organization, deprovisioning processes ensure that unnecessary access is revoked in a timely manner, reducing the risk of insider threats and unauthorized account use.

One of the primary goals of IGA is to enforce the principle of least privilege, ensuring that users only have the access necessary to perform their job functions. Over time, employees may accumulate unnecessary permissions due to job changes, temporary assignments, or manual access requests. Without proper oversight, this accumulation can lead to privilege creep, where users maintain access to systems and data they no longer need. IGA solutions help mitigate this risk by conducting periodic access reviews, allowing managers and security teams to evaluate and revoke excessive permissions. Automated role-based access control (RBAC) and attribute-based access control (ABAC) models further enhance governance by ensuring that access is granted based on structured policies rather than ad hoc decisions.

Compliance is a major driver for organizations implementing IGA, as regulatory frameworks such as GDPR, HIPAA, SOX, and PCI-DSS require strict controls over identity and access management. These regulations mandate that organizations maintain visibility into user access, enforce segregation of duties (SoD), and conduct regular audits to ensure compliance with security policies. IGA solutions provide reporting and audit capabilities that allow organizations to generate detailed access logs, monitor policy violations, and demonstrate compliance during regulatory audits. By maintaining a clear and documented record of identity-related activities, organizations can reduce the risk of compliance failures and associated penalties.

Access request management is another critical aspect of IGA, allowing users to request access to applications and data through a structured approval process. Instead of relying on IT administrators to manually grant permissions, IGA platforms enable self-service access requests with built-in workflows for approval and validation. These workflows may require managerial approval, risk assessments, or additional authentication steps based on the sensitivity of the requested access. By implementing automated access request management, organizations can improve efficiency while maintaining control over who gains access to critical resources.

Risk-based identity governance enhances traditional IGA approaches by incorporating risk analysis and anomaly detection into access management decisions. By leveraging artificial intelligence (AI) and machine learning (ML), IGA solutions can assess user behavior, detect unusual access patterns, and identify potential security risks in real-time. For example, if an employee attempts to access a high-risk application from an unrecognized device or geographic location, the system may trigger an additional authentication step or deny access altogether. This adaptive approach helps organizations proactively manage identity risks and prevent unauthorized access before it leads to a security incident.

IGA also plays a crucial role in managing third-party identities, such as contractors, vendors, and business partners who require temporary access to corporate systems. Unlike full-time employees, third-party users often require access for a limited duration, and failing to properly govern their accounts can result in prolonged access beyond their required timeframe. IGA solutions enforce time-bound access policies, automatically revoking permissions when access is no longer needed.

Additionally, periodic access certifications ensure that managers review and approve ongoing access for third-party users, reducing the risk of orphaned accounts and external threats.

The integration of IGA with cloud environments is becoming increasingly important as organizations adopt hybrid and multi-cloud strategies. Managing identities across on-premises systems and cloud platforms presents new challenges, as traditional access controls may not scale effectively in distributed environments. Modern IGA solutions support cloud-based identity management, enabling organizations to enforce consistent access policies across both on-premises and cloud applications. By leveraging identity federation, single sign-on (SSO), and cloud-based IAM platforms, organizations can streamline identity governance while maintaining security and compliance in cloud ecosystems.

IGA frameworks also facilitate security incident response by providing real-time visibility into user access activities. When a security breach or insider threat is detected, security teams can quickly assess the impacted accounts, revoke access, and initiate forensic investigations using detailed identity logs. This rapid response capability minimizes the potential damage caused by compromised accounts and strengthens the organization's overall cybersecurity posture.

As identity-related threats continue to evolve, the need for strong identity governance and administration practices is more critical than ever. Organizations must adopt a proactive approach to managing identities, enforcing access policies, and monitoring compliance to safeguard their digital assets. By implementing robust IGA solutions, businesses can enhance security, reduce operational inefficiencies, and ensure that their identity management practices align with regulatory and business requirements. The ability to automate identity processes, enforce least privilege access, and detect anomalous behavior positions IGA as a foundational component of modern cybersecurity and risk management strategies.

The Joiner-Mover-Leaver (JML) Process

The Joiner-Mover-Leaver (JML) process is a fundamental framework in identity lifecycle management, ensuring that user access is properly provisioned, maintained, and revoked throughout an individual's tenure within an organization. As businesses grow and evolve, employees, contractors, and third-party users frequently enter, change roles, or exit the organization. Without a structured JML process, managing user identities becomes inefficient, leading to security risks such as unauthorized access, privilege creep, and orphaned accounts. Implementing an effective JML process is essential for security, operational efficiency, and regulatory compliance.

The joiner phase represents the onboarding of a new employee, contractor, or business partner who requires access to corporate systems and applications. This stage begins when an individual is hired or engaged and requires a digital identity to interact with enterprise resources. Traditionally, provisioning user access was a manual process, requiring IT administrators to create accounts, assign permissions, and configure necessary tools. However, manual provisioning is time-consuming, error-prone, and inconsistent across different departments and applications.

Modern organizations leverage automation and identity and access management (IAM) solutions to streamline the joiner process. By integrating HR systems with IAM platforms, new hires can be provisioned automatically based on their job role, department, and location. Role-based access control (RBAC) and attribute-based access control (ABAC) policies define the permissions granted to each user, ensuring they receive the appropriate level of access from day one. Automated provisioning eliminates delays, enhances productivity, and minimizes security risks associated with improper access assignments.

During onboarding, additional security measures such as multi-factor authentication (MFA) and identity verification help ensure that the new joiner's identity is legitimate before granting access. Organizations may also implement just-in-time (JIT) provisioning, which creates user accounts only when access is requested, reducing unnecessary account persistence. Furthermore, training on security policies and access management best practices is often included in the onboarding process to educate new users on their responsibilities in maintaining a secure environment.

The mover phase occurs when an individual changes roles, departments, or responsibilities within the organization. Employees may be promoted, transferred to different teams, or assigned temporary duties that require modified access privileges. Without a well-defined mover process, users may retain access to resources that are no longer relevant to their new roles, leading to privilege creep. Accumulated permissions create security vulnerabilities, increasing the risk of data breaches and insider threats.

A robust mover process ensures that access rights are updated dynamically to reflect job changes. IAM solutions play a crucial role in automating access modifications based on HR updates. When an employee's role changes in the HR system, their access permissions should automatically adjust according to predefined policies. This ensures that users only retain access to the resources necessary for their new responsibilities while revoking outdated permissions.

To further enhance security, organizations conduct periodic access reviews to verify that employees maintain appropriate access levels. Managers and system owners review user entitlements, approving or revoking access as needed. Automated access certification processes streamline this review, providing a structured approach to managing user transitions while maintaining compliance with security policies and regulatory requirements.

The leaver phase is one of the most critical stages in the JML process, as it involves deprovisioning user access when an individual leaves the organization. Departing employees, contractors, or vendors must have their access rights revoked promptly to prevent unauthorized use of corporate systems. Delayed or incomplete deprovisioning can result in orphaned accounts—active accounts belonging to former users that no longer have a legitimate owner. These accounts pose a serious security risk, as they can be exploited by attackers to gain unauthorized entry into corporate networks.

Automated deprovisioning ensures that access is revoked in real-time when an employee's departure is recorded in the HR system. IAM solutions integrate with directory services, cloud platforms, and enterprise applications to deactivate accounts, remove access privileges, and enforce policy-based restrictions. Organizations may implement staged deprovisioning, where immediate removal of critical access is followed by a phased revocation of non-essential services, allowing for an orderly transition.

For high-risk users, such as privileged administrators or employees with access to sensitive data, enhanced security measures during the leaver phase may include immediate session termination, forensic analysis of recent activities, and disabling remote access capabilities. Organizations also conduct exit interviews to recover company-issued devices, revoke physical access to office premises, and remind departing users of confidentiality agreements.

Regulatory compliance plays a significant role in shaping JML processes, as many data protection laws require organizations to maintain strict control over user access. Regulations such as GDPR, HIPAA, and SOX mandate that companies enforce identity governance policies, ensuring that access is granted and revoked appropriately. Auditable JML processes help organizations demonstrate compliance by maintaining records of access changes, approvals, and policy enforcement actions.

The effectiveness of the JML process depends on continuous monitoring, process optimization, and integration with evolving identity management technologies. Organizations adopt artificial intelligence (AI) and machine learning (ML) to enhance JML efficiency, detecting anomalies in user behavior and identifying access risks in real-time. Adaptive identity governance further refines the JML framework by dynamically adjusting access permissions based on user behavior, risk assessments, and contextual factors.

As organizations embrace remote work, cloud-based applications, and hybrid IT environments, the complexity of managing user identities continues to increase. The JML process remains a cornerstone of identity lifecycle management, ensuring that users gain the right access at the right time while preventing security risks associated with excessive or lingering permissions. By implementing automated JML workflows, enforcing access policies, and conducting regular audits, organizations strengthen their identity security posture while enhancing operational efficiency.

Managing User Entitlements and Permissions

Managing user entitlements and permissions is a critical aspect of identity and access management (IAM), ensuring that users have the necessary access to perform their job functions while preventing excessive or unauthorized privileges. Organizations must establish structured access control mechanisms to protect sensitive data, enforce security policies, and comply with regulatory requirements. Without a proper entitlement management framework, businesses face risks such as privilege creep, insider threats, and compliance violations that could lead to financial and reputational damage.

User entitlements define the specific resources, applications, and data that an individual can access within an organization. These entitlements are assigned based on business roles, job responsibilities, and security policies. Permissions, on the other hand, dictate the level of access granted to a user, such as read, write, edit, or delete capabilities. Effective entitlement management ensures that users receive the right level of access at the right time, preventing unauthorized modifications to critical systems and data.

One of the most significant challenges in managing user entitlements is preventing excessive access. Over time, employees may accumulate permissions due to job changes, project assignments, or temporary access grants. If these permissions are not regularly reviewed and revoked when no longer needed, users may retain unnecessary access, creating a security risk known as privilege creep. Attackers can exploit these excessive permissions to escalate privileges, move laterally within a network, or access sensitive information. Organizations must implement policies that enforce the principle of least privilege, ensuring that users only have the access required to perform their duties.

Role-based access control (RBAC) is a common approach used to manage entitlements efficiently. In an RBAC system, users are assigned roles that define their access permissions based on their job functions. This structured approach simplifies access management by grouping permissions into roles instead of assigning them individually. For example, all employees in the finance department may be granted a "Finance Analyst" role, which includes access to accounting software and financial records. If an employee transfers to a different department, their role is updated, automatically modifying their permissions to reflect the new responsibilities.

Attribute-based access control (ABAC) provides a more dynamic method for managing user entitlements by evaluating multiple attributes to determine access decisions. ABAC considers user attributes such as job title, location, department, and security clearance, as well as resource attributes like data classification and access sensitivity. This approach allows organizations to implement fine-grained access policies, ensuring that entitlements align with real-time business and security requirements. For instance, an employee may be permitted to access sensitive documents only from a corporate-issued device within a designated office location but denied access if attempting to log in from an untrusted network.

Regular entitlement reviews are essential to maintaining an effective access management strategy. Organizations must conduct periodic audits to assess whether users still require their assigned permissions. Access certification campaigns involve managers, system owners, and compliance teams reviewing and approving or revoking access based on business needs. These reviews help identify unnecessary entitlements, orphaned accounts, and potential policy violations that could expose the organization to security threats. Automating access reviews with IAM solutions improves efficiency, reduces administrative burden, and ensures continuous compliance with security policies.

Entitlement management is also a key factor in regulatory compliance. Many industry regulations, such as GDPR, HIPAA, and SOX, require organizations to enforce strict access controls, maintain audit trails, and demonstrate accountability for user permissions. Failure to manage entitlements properly can result in non-compliance, leading to financial penalties and legal consequences. IAM platforms provide reporting and monitoring capabilities that help organizations track entitlement changes, detect anomalies, and generate compliance documentation to satisfy regulatory requirements.

Access request management is another important aspect of entitlement governance. Organizations must establish controlled workflows for granting and revoking permissions based on business justification and risk assessment. Self-service access request portals allow users to request entitlements through an approval process involving managers and security teams. This structured approach prevents unauthorized access while providing users with a seamless experience in obtaining necessary permissions. Implementing risk-based access approval mechanisms enhances security by requiring additional verification steps for high-risk requests, such as access to sensitive data or privileged accounts.

Managing privileged entitlements requires additional safeguards to prevent misuse and insider threats. Privileged accounts, such as administrator or superuser accounts, have elevated permissions that grant them control over critical IT infrastructure. Organizations must implement privileged access management (PAM) solutions to enforce strict access controls, monitor privileged sessions, and require multi-factor authentication (MFA) for high-risk actions. Temporary privileged access, known as just-in-time (JIT) provisioning, further reduces security risks by granting administrative permissions only for a limited period before automatically revoking them.

Entitlement enforcement should extend beyond traditional on-premises environments to cloud platforms and third-party applications. With the growing adoption of cloud services, organizations must manage entitlements across hybrid and multi-cloud infrastructures. Cloud-based IAM solutions integrate with software-as-a-service (SaaS) applications, enabling centralized control over user permissions. Identity federation mechanisms, such as single sign-on (SSO) and OAuth-based authorization, streamline entitlement management by allowing users to authenticate once and access multiple cloud resources without repeated logins.

As organizations embrace remote work and digital transformation, entitlement management must adapt to evolving security challenges. Identity analytics and artificial intelligence (AI) enhance entitlement governance by detecting anomalous access patterns, identifying excessive permissions, and recommending access optimization measures. AI-driven insights help security teams proactively manage entitlements, reducing the risk of insider threats and minimizing access-related security incidents.

The ability to manage user entitlements effectively is a fundamental requirement for securing enterprise resources, protecting sensitive data, and ensuring compliance with regulatory mandates. Organizations that implement structured entitlement policies, leverage automation, and enforce least privilege access can significantly reduce the risks associated with excessive permissions. As access requirements continue to evolve, entitlement management remains a cornerstone of identity security, helping businesses maintain control over who can access critical systems and data while enabling operational efficiency.

Identity Reconciliation and Data Synchronization

Identity reconciliation and data synchronization are essential processes in identity and access management (IAM), ensuring that user identities, attributes, and access rights remain consistent across various systems, applications, and directories. As organizations expand their IT environments across on-premises, cloud, and hybrid platforms, managing identities becomes increasingly complex. Without effective reconciliation and synchronization mechanisms, discrepancies in identity data can lead to security risks, compliance violations, and operational inefficiencies. Establishing a structured approach to identity reconciliation and data synchronization helps maintain data integrity, improve security posture, and enhance user experience.

Identity reconciliation involves comparing identity data across multiple sources, detecting inconsistencies, and resolving conflicts to maintain accurate records. Organizations typically store identity data in multiple repositories, including HR databases, directory services, enterprise applications, and cloud platforms. Over time, inconsistencies can arise due to changes in user attributes, delayed updates, or manual errors. If these discrepancies are not addressed, users may retain outdated access privileges, inactive accounts may persist, and identity-related risks may increase. Identity reconciliation ensures that data remains aligned across all systems, reducing the likelihood of unauthorized access and compliance failures.

Data synchronization complements reconciliation by ensuring that identity attributes and access rights are consistently updated across different platforms in real time or at scheduled intervals. Synchronization processes propagate changes in user status, role assignments, and permission modifications across interconnected systems. For example, when an employee's job title changes in an HR system, synchronization ensures that the update is reflected in all relevant identity stores, such as email systems, cloud applications, and access control lists. Automated synchronization eliminates the need for manual intervention, reducing administrative workload while maintaining data consistency.

A common challenge in identity reconciliation is managing duplicate or conflicting identities. When users exist in multiple systems with varying identity records, inconsistencies can lead to access issues or security vulnerabilities. Duplicate identities may arise when an employee receives a new account without deactivating their previous one, resulting in multiple records with different attributes. To address this challenge, organizations implement identity correlation techniques that link accounts belonging to the same individual across different systems. Unique identifiers, such as employee IDs, email addresses, or biometric attributes, help establish identity relationships and resolve duplicate records.

Identity reconciliation plays a crucial role in user provisioning and deprovisioning processes. When a new user is onboarded, reconciliation verifies that no existing identity records conflict with the newly created account. During deprovisioning, reconciliation ensures that all instances of the user's access rights are revoked across all connected systems. Failure to properly reconcile identity data during deprovisioning can result in orphaned accounts, which pose a significant security risk if exploited by malicious actors. Automating identity reconciliation in conjunction with access reviews enhances security by preventing unauthorized retention of privileges.

Effective reconciliation and synchronization require integration between IAM solutions, HR systems, directory services, and cloud platforms. Identity governance frameworks facilitate this integration by defining policies for data consistency and access control. Organizations leverage IAM tools that support real-time data synchronization, ensuring that identity updates propagate instantly across all systems. When identity changes occur, event-driven synchronization mechanisms trigger updates without requiring manual input, reducing the risk of outdated access records.

Data synchronization must also account for latency and system dependencies. Some enterprise applications and legacy systems may not support real-time synchronization, requiring batch updates at predefined intervals. Organizations implement scheduled synchronization processes to accommodate such systems, ensuring that identity data remains consistent while minimizing disruptions. However, batch synchronization introduces challenges related to data staleness, as updates may not immediately reflect changes in user status. Hybrid synchronization strategies, combining real-time and scheduled updates, provide a balanced approach to maintaining identity accuracy.

Security considerations are critical when implementing identity reconciliation and data synchronization. Ensuring data integrity, preventing unauthorized modifications, and securing data transmission are essential to maintaining a robust IAM framework. Encryption, access controls, and logging mechanisms safeguard identity data as it moves between systems. Organizations also enforce role-based access control (RBAC) and attribute-based access control (ABAC) policies to restrict access to identity data based on job responsibilities and security clearance levels.

Compliance requirements further emphasize the importance of identity reconciliation and data synchronization. Regulations such as GDPR, HIPAA, and SOX mandate strict controls over identity data management, requiring organizations to maintain accurate records and ensure timely updates. IAM solutions with built-in audit capabilities help organizations track identity changes, generate compliance reports, and demonstrate adherence to regulatory standards. Automated reconciliation and synchronization reduce the risk of non-compliance by ensuring that access records are continuously updated and aligned with policy requirements.

Organizations adopting cloud-based identity services face additional challenges in maintaining identity consistency across hybrid environments. Cloud identity providers, such as Azure AD, Okta, and AWS IAM, must synchronize user identities with on-premises directories, SaaS applications, and third-party systems. Federated identity management solutions enable seamless identity synchronization across different platforms, ensuring that users can authenticate consistently across all connected services. Cloud-based synchronization solutions leverage APIs and identity federation protocols, such as SAML and OpenID Connect, to facilitate real-time updates and secure identity transactions.

As organizations continue to expand their digital ecosystems, the complexity of managing identity data will increase. Implementing scalable identity reconciliation and synchronization strategies is essential for maintaining security, efficiency, and compliance. By leveraging automation, integrating IAM solutions with business applications, and enforcing identity governance policies, organizations can ensure that identity data remains accurate and consistent across all systems. The ability to reconcile and synchronize identity information effectively enhances operational agility, reduces security risks, and supports digital transformation initiatives.

Identity Lifecycle in Cloud Environments

The shift to cloud environments has transformed the way organizations manage user identities, access controls, and security policies. Identity lifecycle management, which governs the creation, modification, and termination of user accounts, has become more complex as businesses move workloads to cloud platforms. Unlike traditional on-premises environments, where identities are typically managed through centralized directory services, cloud environments introduce distributed identity ecosystems that span multiple providers, applications, and geographic locations. Effective identity lifecycle management in the cloud requires automation, integration, and governance to ensure security, efficiency, and compliance.

User provisioning in cloud environments is often handled through identity-as-a-service (IDaaS) platforms, which provide centralized identity management for cloud-based applications. When a new user joins an organization, their identity must be provisioned across multiple cloud services, such as SaaS applications, cloud-based collaboration tools, and virtual infrastructure platforms. Unlike legacy provisioning processes that rely on manual account creation, cloud identity lifecycle management leverages APIs, identity synchronization, and automated workflows to streamline provisioning. By integrating cloud IAM solutions with HR systems and directory services, organizations can ensure that new users receive the appropriate access rights from the moment they are onboarded.

Cloud identity lifecycle management must also account for dynamic user roles and attribute-based access requirements. Unlike static access control models, which assign permissions based on predefined roles, cloud environments benefit from attribute-based access control (ABAC), where access is determined based on contextual factors such as job function, device type, and location. This approach enables organizations to enforce least privilege access in cloud ecosystems, granting users only the permissions necessary to perform their duties. Additionally, identity federation allows users to authenticate across multiple cloud applications using a single set of credentials, reducing password sprawl and improving security.

One of the key challenges in managing identity lifecycles in the cloud is handling user mobility. Employees frequently access cloud applications from different devices, networks, and geographic locations, requiring adaptive authentication mechanisms to verify their identities. Cloud IAM solutions implement risk-based authentication, which evaluates contextual signals such as login location, device health, and access patterns to determine the appropriate authentication method. If an access request originates from an unfamiliar location or device, additional authentication steps, such as multi-factor authentication (MFA), may be required to verify the user's identity before granting access.

Identity lifecycle management in the cloud must also address the complexities of role transitions. Employees change roles, take on temporary assignments, and participate in cross-functional projects that require access to different cloud applications. Without proper lifecycle controls, users may retain unnecessary permissions, leading to privilege creep. Automated role management and access certification processes help organizations enforce timely access changes. When an employee transitions to a new role, cloud IAM solutions can dynamically update their permissions, ensuring that they no longer have access to resources associated with their previous position. Periodic access reviews further reduce the risk of excessive entitlements by enabling managers to validate and approve current access rights.

User deprovisioning in cloud environments presents unique security risks if not handled properly. When an employee leaves an organization, their access must be revoked across all cloud services to prevent unauthorized use of corporate data and applications. Unlike on-premises environments, where access can be centrally managed through Active Directory, cloud environments require organizations to track and disable accounts across multiple service providers. Cloud IAM solutions automate deprovisioning by integrating with HR systems and cloud directories to disable accounts, revoke API keys, and terminate active sessions in real time. Failure to properly deprovision users in cloud environments increases the risk of orphaned accounts, which can be exploited by malicious actors.

Managing machine identities and service accounts is another critical aspect of cloud identity lifecycle management. Cloud environments rely heavily on non-human identities, such as API keys, service accounts, and containerized workloads, to facilitate automation and integration between cloud services. Unlike human identities, which follow a predictable lifecycle of onboarding, role transitions, and deprovisioning, machine identities require continuous lifecycle monitoring to prevent security vulnerabilities. Organizations must implement policies for rotating API keys, restricting service account permissions, and enforcing least privilege access to minimize the risk of credential leaks and unauthorized access to cloud resources.

Cloud environments also introduce new compliance challenges for identity lifecycle management. Organizations must ensure that identity governance policies align with industry regulations such as GDPR, HIPAA, and SOC 2, which mandate strict controls over user access and data protection. Cloud IAM solutions provide audit logging and reporting capabilities to track identity lifecycle events, such as account provisioning, access modifications, and deprovisioning.

Automated compliance workflows help organizations enforce policies by flagging access anomalies, detecting policy violations, and generating compliance reports for regulatory audits.

Hybrid and multi-cloud strategies further complicate identity lifecycle management by introducing multiple identity providers and authentication mechanisms. Organizations operating in multi-cloud environments must establish a unified identity strategy to ensure consistency across different cloud platforms. Identity federation and single sign-on (SSO) enable users to authenticate seamlessly across cloud services without managing multiple credentials. Additionally, organizations leverage cloud access security brokers (CASBs) to monitor and enforce identity policies across cloud applications, mitigating the risk of unauthorized access and data leakage.

As cloud adoption continues to grow, identity lifecycle management must evolve to support new technologies, security threats, and regulatory requirements. Organizations increasingly rely on artificial intelligence (AI) and machine learning (ML) to enhance identity governance, detecting anomalous access patterns and predicting potential security risks. By analyzing user behavior, AI-driven identity analytics help organizations proactively enforce identity policies, detect insider threats, and optimize access controls in cloud environments.

The complexity of identity lifecycle management in cloud environments requires organizations to adopt a proactive approach that integrates automation, governance, and security best practices. By leveraging cloud IAM solutions, enforcing attribute-based access controls, and continuously monitoring identity-related activities, organizations can ensure that user identities are managed efficiently while maintaining security, compliance, and operational agility. Cloud identity lifecycle management remains a cornerstone of modern cybersecurity strategies, providing the foundation for secure digital transformation and seamless cloud adoption.

Multi-Factor Authentication (MFA) and Identity Verification

Multi-Factor Authentication (MFA) and identity verification are essential components of modern cybersecurity, ensuring that users prove their identities before accessing sensitive systems and data. As cyber threats evolve, relying on traditional username and password authentication is no longer sufficient. Passwords are vulnerable to phishing, brute-force attacks, and credential stuffing, making them a weak point in security strategies. MFA enhances authentication security by requiring users to provide multiple forms of verification before gaining access. This additional layer of protection significantly reduces the risk of unauthorized access, even if a password is compromised.

MFA operates by requiring two or more authentication factors from different categories: something the user knows, something the user has, and something the user is. The knowledge factor typically includes passwords, PINs, or security questions. The possession factor involves physical or digital items such as mobile authentication apps, security tokens, or smart cards. The inherence factor relies on biometric data, such as fingerprints, facial recognition, or voice patterns. By combining these factors, MFA ensures that attackers cannot access an account using stolen credentials alone.

Identity verification plays a critical role in establishing trust before granting access to sensitive systems. Unlike authentication, which confirms that a user is who they claim to be at the moment of login, identity verification is the process of proving an individual's identity during onboarding or high-risk transactions. Verification methods include document-based verification, knowledge-based authentication (KBA), and biometric verification. Organizations often require identity verification when registering new employees, customers, or business partners, ensuring that the provided credentials belong to a legitimate individual.

The adoption of MFA has increased due to rising cybersecurity threats, regulatory requirements, and industry best practices. Many organizations enforce MFA policies to comply with data protection regulations such as GDPR, HIPAA, and PCI-DSS. Financial institutions, healthcare providers, and government agencies require MFA to secure online transactions, protect sensitive information, and prevent fraud. Regulatory frameworks often mandate the use of MFA for remote access, privileged accounts, and high-risk operations to mitigate security threats.

MFA deployment varies depending on organizational needs and user experience considerations. Some implementations use time-based one-time passwords (TOTP), where users generate temporary authentication codes from mobile applications such as Google Authenticator or Microsoft Authenticator. Push notifications provide a more seamless MFA experience, allowing users to approve login requests on their mobile devices. Hardware security keys, such as YubiKeys, offer strong security by requiring physical possession of a device for authentication. Organizations must balance security and usability when implementing MFA, ensuring that authentication methods do not create unnecessary friction for users.

Adaptive authentication enhances MFA by assessing risk factors in real time before determining the required authentication level. Instead of enforcing strict MFA policies for all users, adaptive authentication analyzes contextual signals such as device reputation, geographic location, and login behavior to decide whether additional verification is necessary. If a user logs in from a trusted device and location, standard authentication may suffice. However, if the same user attempts to access an account from an unfamiliar IP address or unusual time zone, the system may prompt for additional authentication factors. This risk-based approach improves security without introducing excessive authentication steps for low-risk activities.

Biometric authentication has gained popularity as a secure and convenient MFA method. Fingerprint scanning, facial recognition, and iris scanning provide unique identifiers that are difficult to replicate. Many modern devices, including smartphones and laptops, support biometric authentication, allowing users to log in without remembering passwords. However, biometric data requires careful handling, as compromised biometric information cannot be changed like passwords. Organizations implementing biometric authentication must use encryption, secure storage, and privacy-preserving techniques to protect biometric data from misuse.

Despite the benefits of MFA, attackers continue to develop sophisticated techniques to bypass authentication mechanisms. Phishing-resistant MFA methods, such as FIDO2-based authentication, address these challenges by eliminating reliance on passwords and one-time codes. FIDO2 security keys leverage public-key cryptography to authenticate users securely without transmitting sensitive credentials. This approach prevents common attacks, such as phishing and man-in-the-middle (MITM) attacks, by ensuring that authentication occurs only on legitimate websites and applications.

Identity verification remains essential for account recovery and fraud prevention. Organizations must implement secure verification processes to prevent unauthorized account takeovers. Self-service account recovery workflows often require users to verify their identity using previously registered authentication factors. High-security environments may require manual identity verification, where users provide government-issued identification or undergo video verification. Strengthening identity verification processes reduces the risk of social engineering attacks that exploit weak recovery mechanisms.

Cloud-based MFA solutions enable organizations to extend authentication security across multiple applications and environments. Identity providers (IdPs) such as Microsoft Azure AD, Okta, and Google Identity Platform offer centralized authentication services that integrate with enterprise applications, SaaS platforms, and cloud services. By enforcing MFA policies at the identity provider level, organizations can secure access to multiple resources without requiring users to manage separate authentication methods for each application. Single Sign-On (SSO) combined with MFA improves security and user experience by allowing seamless authentication across connected services.

Organizations must educate users about the importance of MFA and identity verification to ensure widespread adoption. Security awareness training helps employees recognize phishing attempts, avoid credential reuse, and understand the risks of weak authentication practices. Encouraging users to enable MFA for personal accounts, such as email and social media, reinforces cybersecurity best practices beyond the workplace. Organizations should also provide support for users who encounter difficulties with authentication, ensuring that security measures do not hinder productivity.

The future of MFA and identity verification will continue evolving with advancements in authentication technologies, artificial intelligence, and decentralized identity models. AI-driven authentication enhances security by analyzing behavioral patterns and detecting anomalies in authentication attempts. Decentralized identity solutions, built on blockchain technology, aim to give users control over their personal information while enabling secure identity verification. As cyber threats become more sophisticated, organizations must continually adapt authentication strategies to protect users, data, and digital assets from unauthorized access.

Single Sign-On (SSO) and Federation

Single Sign-On (SSO) and federation are critical components of modern identity and access management (IAM), enabling users to authenticate once and gain access to multiple applications without needing to log in separately for each service. As organizations adopt cloud services, enterprise applications, and hybrid IT environments, managing multiple credentials for different systems becomes inefficient and insecure. SSO and federation streamline authentication processes, enhance security, and improve user experience by reducing the need for repeated logins while maintaining strong access control policies.

SSO allows users to log in once with a single set of credentials and gain access to multiple interconnected applications and services. This eliminates the need for users to remember and enter multiple usernames and passwords, reducing password fatigue and the risk of password-related security breaches. Organizations implementing SSO typically use identity providers (IdPs) to authenticate users centrally and then grant access to various applications based on established trust relationships. Common IdPs include Microsoft Azure AD, Okta,

Google Identity Platform, and Ping Identity, which facilitate seamless authentication across enterprise and cloud environments.

Security is a primary advantage of SSO, as it minimizes the risk of weak passwords being used across different applications. When users are required to maintain separate passwords for multiple systems, they often resort to reusing passwords or choosing weak credentials that are easy to remember but also easy to compromise. SSO reduces this risk by requiring only one strong authentication process, often combined with multi-factor authentication (MFA) for enhanced security. By centralizing authentication, organizations can enforce strong password policies, monitor login attempts, and detect suspicious activities more effectively.

Another benefit of SSO is improved user experience and productivity. Employees, partners, and customers can access business applications without interruptions, reducing login friction and eliminating the need to reset forgotten passwords frequently. In large enterprises with multiple applications, SSO simplifies IT operations by reducing help desk requests related to password resets and access issues. This efficiency translates into cost savings, as IT teams spend less time managing user credentials and resolving authentication-related problems.

Federation extends the capabilities of SSO by enabling authentication and authorization across multiple organizations, domains, or service providers. In a federated identity model, users can authenticate with one organization and access resources from another trusted organization without needing to create separate credentials. This is particularly useful for businesses collaborating with external partners, cloud service providers, and third-party applications. Federation relies on trust relationships established through identity federation protocols, such as Security Assertion Markup Language (SAML), OpenID Connect (OIDC), and OAuth 2.0.

SAML is a widely used federation protocol that enables secure authentication and authorization between identity providers and service providers. When a user attempts to access a federated service, the service provider redirects them to the identity provider for authentication. Upon successful authentication, the identity provider issues a SAML assertion containing user identity details, which the service provider uses to grant access. This mechanism ensures that credentials remain within the identity provider's domain, reducing the risk of password exposure and unauthorized access.

OpenID Connect (OIDC) is another popular federation protocol built on top of OAuth 2.0, designed for modern web and mobile applications. OIDC allows applications to verify a user's identity through an identity provider, using access tokens and ID tokens to facilitate authentication. Unlike SAML, which primarily targets enterprise environments, OIDC is widely used for consumer-facing applications, social logins, and API security. Many major identity providers, including Google, Microsoft, and Facebook, support OIDC, allowing users to authenticate with their existing credentials across various online services.

OAuth 2.0 plays a crucial role in identity federation by enabling secure authorization without exposing user credentials. OAuth 2.0 allows users to grant third-party applications limited access to their resources without sharing their passwords. For example, a user can log into a third-party application using their Google or Microsoft account, granting access to specific data while maintaining control over their credentials. OAuth-based authorization flows, such as Authorization Code Flow and Client Credentials Flow, enable seamless authentication and delegated access management for cloud services and APIs.

Federated identity management benefits organizations that operate in multi-cloud environments, partner ecosystems, and digital supply chains. Enterprises using multiple cloud service providers can implement federation to unify authentication across platforms such as AWS, Microsoft Azure, and Google Cloud. By establishing trust between identity providers and service providers, federation reduces the complexity of managing multiple identities and access controls across different cloud ecosystems.

Security considerations play a critical role in SSO and federation implementations. While SSO enhances security by reducing password usage, it also introduces a single point of failure. If an attacker compromises an SSO account, they may gain access to multiple applications and systems. To mitigate this risk, organizations enforce MFA, risk-based authentication, and anomaly detection to strengthen security controls. Monitoring user activity, implementing session timeouts, and restricting access based on contextual factors such as device and location further enhance protection.

Federation also requires careful governance to maintain trust relationships between identity providers and service providers. Organizations must establish clear identity federation policies, ensuring that only authorized users and trusted entities participate in federated authentication. Regular audits, certificate management, and security assessments help maintain integrity and prevent misuse of federated identities.

As organizations continue to adopt cloud-based services, hybrid IT infrastructures, and digital collaboration platforms, the demand for SSO and federation will grow. Businesses seek seamless authentication experiences while maintaining strong security controls, regulatory compliance, and operational efficiency. Emerging technologies such as decentralized identity and blockchain-based authentication may further enhance SSO and federation by providing users with greater control over their digital identities while reducing reliance on centralized identity providers.

The role of SSO and federation in modern IAM strategies is increasingly important as organizations navigate complex identity ecosystems. By leveraging identity federation protocols, enforcing strong authentication mechanisms, and integrating with cloud-based identity solutions, businesses can provide secure, seamless access to applications while protecting user identities and reducing security risks. The ongoing evolution of authentication technologies and federation standards will shape the future of identity management, enabling organizations to adopt scalable, secure, and user-friendly authentication solutions across their digital environments.

Managing Privileged Access and Admin Accounts

Managing privileged access and admin accounts is a critical aspect of identity and access management (IAM), ensuring that highly sensitive credentials and administrative privileges are protected from misuse, insider threats, and external cyberattacks. Privileged accounts have elevated permissions that allow users to make critical system changes, access confidential data, and manage IT infrastructure. Without proper governance, these accounts become prime targets for cybercriminals seeking to exploit security gaps and gain unauthorized access to enterprise systems. Implementing strong privileged access management (PAM) strategies helps organizations secure administrative credentials, enforce least privilege policies, and reduce the risk of privilege escalation attacks.

Privileged accounts exist in various forms, including system administrator accounts, domain administrator accounts, root accounts, service accounts, and application credentials. These accounts often have extensive permissions that, if compromised, could lead to devastating consequences such as data breaches, ransomware attacks, and operational disruptions. Traditional access control methods are insufficient for managing privileged accounts due to their elevated risks, requiring specialized security controls to prevent unauthorized use. Organizations must implement strict policies to regulate how privileged access is granted, monitored, and revoked to maintain a secure IT environment.

A key principle in managing privileged access is enforcing the least privilege model, which ensures that users receive only the minimum level of access required to perform their tasks. Granting broad administrative privileges to multiple users increases the attack surface and elevates the risk of insider threats. Instead of providing permanent administrative access, organizations should implement just-in-time (JIT) access controls, which grant temporary privileges only when necessary. JIT access reduces the exposure of privileged credentials and minimizes the risk of unauthorized modifications to critical systems.

Privileged access management solutions provide a centralized framework for securing and controlling administrative credentials. These solutions include password vaulting, session monitoring, and privilege elevation controls that help organizations manage and secure privileged accounts. Password vaults store administrator credentials in a secure, encrypted repository, preventing users from accessing them directly. Instead of manually entering passwords, authorized users retrieve credentials through automated workflows that enforce security policies, such as requiring multi-factor authentication (MFA) and approval from designated approvers.

Session monitoring and recording are essential components of privileged access security, allowing organizations to track administrative actions in real time. PAM solutions capture privileged session activity, recording keystrokes, commands, and system changes for audit and compliance purposes. If suspicious behavior is detected, security teams can analyze session logs to investigate potential breaches and respond to security incidents. Real-time session termination capabilities further enhance security by allowing administrators to immediately disconnect unauthorized or high-risk sessions.

Managing service accounts presents unique challenges due to their widespread use in automated processes, system integrations, and application dependencies. Unlike user accounts, service accounts do not have a human owner actively managing them, increasing the risk of mismanagement and security lapses. Many service accounts are created with default or hardcoded credentials that never expire, making them attractive targets for attackers. Organizations must implement automated lifecycle management for service accounts, enforcing regular credential rotation, limiting privileges, and applying least privilege principles to prevent over-permissioned service accounts from being exploited.

Multi-factor authentication plays a crucial role in securing privileged accounts, adding an extra layer of protection against unauthorized access. Requiring privileged users to authenticate using a combination of passwords, biometrics, security tokens, or mobile authenticator apps reduces the risk of credential-based attacks such as phishing and credential stuffing. Implementing risk-based authentication further enhances security by assessing login behaviors, device reputations, and geographic locations to determine whether additional verification is necessary before granting privileged access.

Privileged access governance is a fundamental requirement for compliance with industry regulations such as GDPR, HIPAA, SOX, and NIST. These regulations mandate strict controls over administrative credentials, requiring organizations to maintain visibility into privileged activities, enforce access reviews, and implement audit trails. Regular privileged access reviews help organizations verify that only authorized users retain administrative privileges and ensure that excessive or unnecessary permissions are revoked. Automated PAM solutions streamline compliance by generating detailed reports on privileged access events, providing auditors with visibility into how administrative credentials are managed and used.

Privileged account discovery is an essential first step in securing administrative credentials. Many organizations have undocumented or unmanaged privileged accounts that accumulate over time, increasing the risk of security breaches. PAM tools include discovery capabilities that scan IT environments to identify all privileged accounts, service accounts, and embedded credentials. Once identified, organizations can onboard these accounts into a PAM system, apply security policies, and enforce governance controls to ensure they are properly managed.

Segregation of duties (SoD) is another key principle in privileged access management, preventing conflicts of interest and reducing the risk of insider threats. SoD policies ensure that no single user has complete control over critical processes, such as financial transactions, system configurations, or data access approvals. By dividing administrative responsibilities among multiple users and requiring dual approvals for high-risk activities, organizations can strengthen their security posture and prevent unauthorized changes to sensitive systems.

As organizations transition to cloud environments and adopt hybrid IT infrastructures, privileged access management must evolve to address new security challenges. Cloud service providers, DevOps teams, and remote administrators require privileged access to manage cloud resources, virtual machines, and APIs. Traditional PAM solutions must integrate with cloud IAM platforms to provide seamless privileged access control across on-premises and cloud environments. Implementing cloud-native PAM solutions allows organizations to enforce privilege policies, monitor cloud administrator activities, and secure cloud-based credentials to prevent unauthorized access.

Artificial intelligence and machine learning enhance privileged access management by identifying anomalies in privileged user behavior and detecting potential security threats. AI-driven analytics analyze access patterns, flag unusual activities, and provide risk-based recommendations to security teams. By leveraging AI for privileged access security, organizations can proactively mitigate risks, automate threat detection, and improve response times to potential security incidents.

Organizations must continuously refine their privileged access management strategies to keep pace with evolving cyber threats, regulatory requirements, and technological advancements. By implementing strict privilege controls, enforcing least privilege policies, and leveraging automated PAM solutions, businesses can protect their most sensitive accounts from unauthorized access and ensure the integrity of their IT environments. Effective privileged access management reduces the risk of credential theft, prevents privilege escalation attacks, and strengthens overall cybersecurity defenses, safeguarding enterprise assets from internal and external threats.

Identity Proofing and Onboarding Best Practices

Identity proofing and onboarding are critical steps in establishing trust between users and an organization's digital systems. These processes ensure that individuals are who they claim to be before granting them access to corporate resources, applications, and data. As organizations embrace digital transformation, identity proofing has become more sophisticated, incorporating advanced verification technologies to prevent fraud, reduce security risks, and comply with regulatory requirements. A well-structured onboarding process enhances security while improving the user experience, enabling employees, customers, and partners to gain access to necessary services efficiently.

Identity proofing is the process of verifying a user's identity before granting them access to a system or service. This verification is particularly important for employees, contractors, and external users who require access to sensitive data and applications. Traditional identity proofing methods involve manual document verification, where users submit identification documents such as passports, driver's licenses, or national ID cards. While manual verification can be effective, it is time-consuming and prone to human error. Organizations are increasingly adopting digital identity proofing techniques, leveraging artificial intelligence (AI), biometrics, and data analytics to enhance accuracy and efficiency.

Biometric verification plays a significant role in modern identity proofing. Fingerprint scanning, facial recognition, and iris scanning provide highly secure and convenient authentication methods that reduce the reliance on passwords and traditional credentials. Many organizations integrate biometric verification into their onboarding workflows to enhance security while simplifying the user experience. Unlike passwords, biometric data cannot be easily stolen or shared, making it an effective deterrent against identity fraud and account takeovers.

Knowledge-based authentication (KBA) is another method used in identity proofing, requiring users to answer personal security questions based on information from credit reports, financial transactions, or previous account activity. While KBA has been widely used in financial services and government applications, it has limitations due to the increasing availability of personal data on the dark web. Cybercriminals can obtain answers to security questions through data breaches or social engineering, reducing the effectiveness of KBA in high-risk scenarios.

Document verification technology enhances identity proofing by using optical character recognition (OCR) and AI-powered analysis to validate official identification documents. Users are required to submit a photo of their government-issued ID, which is analyzed for authenticity and matched against databases to confirm legitimacy. Some verification systems incorporate liveness detection, prompting users to take a real-time selfie to ensure that the person submitting the

ID matches the document's photo. These measures prevent fraudsters from using stolen or counterfeit documents to bypass identity checks.

Once identity proofing is complete, the onboarding process determines how efficiently a user gains access to corporate resources. A seamless onboarding experience balances security with convenience, ensuring that legitimate users can quickly access the systems they need without unnecessary friction. Organizations implement automated onboarding workflows that integrate with HR systems, identity and access management (IAM) platforms, and directory services to streamline account creation and access provisioning.

Role-based access control (RBAC) and attribute-based access control (ABAC) help define access permissions during onboarding, ensuring that users receive the appropriate level of access based on their job functions, responsibilities, and security clearance. By assigning access rights dynamically based on predefined rules, organizations reduce the risk of over-provisioning while maintaining operational efficiency. Automated provisioning eliminates manual errors and accelerates the onboarding process, improving productivity for new employees and reducing administrative overhead.

Multi-factor authentication (MFA) enhances security during onboarding by requiring users to verify their identities through multiple authentication factors. Organizations commonly enforce MFA when users access systems for the first time or request elevated privileges. Requiring a combination of a password, biometric verification, or a one-time authentication code strengthens security by preventing unauthorized access. Adaptive authentication further improves security by assessing risk factors, such as device reputation, login location, and network conditions, before determining the level of authentication required.

Self-service onboarding portals improve the user experience by allowing individuals to complete their identity verification and access requests independently. These portals enable users to submit identification documents, set up MFA, and request access to applications without relying on IT administrators. Automated workflows route access requests through approval chains, ensuring that managers and security teams review and authorize access based on predefined policies. Self-service onboarding reduces IT workload while empowering users with greater control over their access needs.

Compliance and regulatory considerations play a significant role in shaping identity proofing and onboarding best practices. Organizations in highly regulated industries, such as finance, healthcare, and government, must adhere to stringent identity verification requirements to prevent fraud and unauthorized access. Regulations such as GDPR, HIPAA, and KYC (Know Your Customer) mandate identity proofing processes to protect sensitive data and prevent money laundering, identity theft, and cybercrime. Maintaining audit trails of onboarding activities ensures transparency and compliance with regulatory standards.

Identity lifecycle management ensures that onboarding processes align with long-term identity governance strategies. Once a user is onboarded, their access must be continuously reviewed and updated to reflect changes in job roles, organizational structure, and security policies. Regular access reviews and automated recertification processes help organizations maintain a secure access environment by revoking unnecessary permissions and enforcing least privilege access.

The adoption of artificial intelligence and machine learning in identity proofing enhances security by detecting anomalies and preventing fraudulent account registrations. AI-powered identity verification solutions analyze behavioral patterns, device fingerprints, and risk signals to identify suspicious activities during onboarding. If an identity verification attempt appears abnormal or high-risk, additional authentication steps or manual review may be required before granting access. These advanced security measures strengthen identity proofing while minimizing friction for legitimate users.

Organizations implementing identity proofing and onboarding best practices must continuously evaluate and improve their processes to address emerging security threats and compliance requirements. As cybercriminals develop more sophisticated identity fraud techniques, businesses must adopt adaptive identity verification solutions that evolve with changing risks. By integrating advanced verification technologies, enforcing strong authentication controls, and optimizing onboarding workflows, organizations can establish a secure and user-friendly identity management framework.

Handling Contractor and Temporary Identities

Managing contractor and temporary identities is a critical aspect of identity and access management (IAM), ensuring that non-permanent users have the appropriate level of access to enterprise resources while minimizing security risks. Contractors, vendors, consultants, and temporary employees often require access to corporate systems, cloud applications, and sensitive data for limited durations. Unlike full-time employees, these users do not follow the same onboarding, provisioning, and deprovisioning lifecycle, making it essential to implement distinct security controls and governance policies. Without proper management, temporary identities can become a significant security vulnerability, leading to excessive permissions, orphaned accounts, and compliance violations.

One of the primary challenges in handling contractor identities is defining the scope of access required for their roles. Organizations must strike a balance between granting necessary access to enable productivity and restricting permissions to reduce exposure to sensitive data. Implementing the principle of least privilege (PoLP) ensures that contractors and temporary users receive only the minimum access required to perform their tasks. Access should be role-based, with predefined permissions assigned according to the nature of the engagement rather than individual user preferences. Temporary accounts should never have permanent administrative privileges, and access should be regularly reviewed to prevent privilege creep.

Onboarding contractors and temporary workers requires an efficient and secure process that differs from full-time employee onboarding. Organizations should leverage automated identity lifecycle management solutions to streamline the provisioning of temporary identities. Integration with human resources (HR) systems, vendor management platforms, and IAM solutions allows for seamless account creation, role assignment, and access approvals. Instead of relying on manual provisioning, automated workflows ensure that contractors are granted access based on predefined policies and that their accounts are automatically deactivated when their contracts end.

Identity verification is a crucial step in onboarding external users, ensuring that only legitimate contractors and temporary employees gain access to corporate systems. Organizations should implement identity proofing techniques such as document verification, biometric authentication, and multi-factor authentication (MFA) to validate user identities before granting access. Temporary identities should be subjected to the same authentication requirements as full-time employees, preventing unauthorized access by attackers posing as contractors or third-party vendors.

Time-based access controls play a vital role in managing temporary identities. Unlike permanent employees, contractors often have fixed engagement periods, requiring access for a specific duration. Organizations should enforce expiration policies that automatically disable temporary accounts at the end of the contract period. Just-in-time (JIT) access provisioning further enhances security by granting access only when needed and revoking it when no longer required. By implementing time-limited access policies, businesses reduce the risk of orphaned accounts and ensure that former contractors do not retain unnecessary permissions.

Segregation of duties (SoD) is essential when handling contractor identities, preventing conflicts of interest and reducing insider threats. Organizations should establish policies that restrict temporary users from accessing critical systems or performing high-risk actions without proper oversight. Contractors should not have access to privileged accounts, financial transactions, or regulatory compliance data unless explicitly required and approved. Dual-approval workflows and access reviews help enforce SoD by requiring managerial or security team authorization before granting elevated privileges.

Monitoring and auditing contractor activity is necessary to detect potential security incidents and ensure compliance with internal policies and regulatory requirements. Organizations should implement real-time logging and session recording for temporary identities, tracking access events, login attempts, and data modifications. Security teams should regularly review logs to identify suspicious behavior, such as unauthorized data downloads, multiple failed login attempts, or access requests outside of normal working hours. By leveraging AI-driven anomaly detection, organizations can proactively identify security threats related to contractor access.

Third-party identity federation simplifies access management for contractors by allowing them to authenticate using their existing credentials from trusted identity providers. Instead of creating separate accounts for each temporary user, organizations can integrate with external identity providers, such as corporate partners or vendor organizations, using Security Assertion Markup Language (SAML) or OpenID Connect (OIDC). This approach reduces administrative overhead while maintaining control over external user access. Federated authentication also improves security by enabling organizations to enforce their own access policies while leveraging external identity validation mechanisms.

Organizations must also establish clear policies for contractor offboarding and access revocation. When a contractor's engagement ends, their accounts must be immediately deactivated, and all access credentials, such as VPN tokens, API keys, and system accounts, should be revoked. Delays in offboarding can lead to security risks, as former contractors may still have active accounts that could be exploited. Automated deprovisioning workflows integrated with contract management systems ensure that accounts are disabled on time, reducing the likelihood of orphaned identities remaining in the system.

Compliance requirements further emphasize the need for strong governance over temporary identities. Regulations such as GDPR, HIPAA, and SOC 2 mandate strict controls over third-party access to sensitive data, requiring organizations to enforce policies that prevent unauthorized access and data misuse. Regular access reviews, policy enforcement mechanisms, and audit trails ensure that contractor identities comply with regulatory standards. Failure to manage temporary identities effectively can lead to non-compliance, exposing organizations to legal penalties and reputational damage.

Managing contractor and temporary identities in cloud environments presents additional challenges, as cloud platforms often provide broad access to distributed resources. Organizations should implement cloud access security broker (CASB) solutions to monitor and enforce security policies for temporary users accessing cloud-based applications. Granular access controls, session-based authentication, and device trust assessments help organizations secure cloud environments while allowing temporary users to perform necessary tasks.

As organizations continue to rely on contractors and temporary workers for specialized projects, short-term engagements, and outsourced tasks, securing temporary identities remains a top priority. Implementing automated onboarding, strict access controls, real-time monitoring, and effective offboarding policies ensures that contractor access is managed securely and efficiently. By applying IAM best practices and leveraging modern security technologies, organizations can protect their digital assets while maintaining operational agility in an evolving workforce landscape.

Service Accounts and Non-Human Identities

Service accounts and non-human identities play a crucial role in modern IT environments, enabling automated processes, applications, and system integrations to function securely and efficiently. Unlike traditional user accounts, these identities do not belong to individual users but are instead associated with software, scripts, application programming interfaces (APIs), containers, and cloud workloads. As organizations increase their reliance on automation, cloud computing, and DevOps methodologies, managing service accounts and non-human identities becomes a critical aspect of identity and access management (IAM). Without proper governance, these accounts can become security vulnerabilities, leading to credential leaks, unauthorized access, and compliance risks.

Service accounts are often used by applications, databases, and IT systems to perform automated tasks, such as running background jobs, accessing network resources, and communicating between different systems. These accounts typically have elevated privileges and persistent access, making them attractive targets for attackers. Unlike user identities, which follow a lifecycle of onboarding, role transitions, and offboarding, service accounts tend to persist indefinitely unless explicitly managed. Organizations must implement strict policies to govern service account provisioning, usage, and deprovisioning to mitigate security risks.

One of the primary challenges in managing service accounts is ensuring that they operate under the principle of least privilege. Many service accounts are over-provisioned, granted broad administrative privileges that exceed their actual requirements. This over-permissioning increases the risk of lateral movement attacks, where compromised service account credentials allow attackers to escalate privileges and move across systems undetected. Organizations must conduct regular access reviews to determine whether service accounts have excessive permissions and revoke unnecessary privileges to limit their potential impact in the event of a breach.

Credential management is a critical aspect of securing service accounts. Unlike user accounts, which often require periodic password changes, service accounts frequently use static credentials that remain unchanged for long periods. Hardcoded credentials, stored in application code, configuration files, or scripts, pose a significant security risk, as they can be inadvertently exposed through code repositories, logging systems, or misconfigured access controls. To mitigate these risks, organizations should implement password vaulting and secrets management solutions to securely store and rotate service account credentials. Automated credential rotation reduces the likelihood of credential compromise while ensuring that applications can continue operating without disruption.

Non-human identities extend beyond traditional service accounts to include robotic process automation (RPA), machine identities, containerized workloads, and Internet of Things (IoT) devices. Each of these identities requires authentication and authorization mechanisms to securely interact with enterprise systems and data. Unlike human users, non-human identities operate at scale, requiring automated provisioning, monitoring, and governance to prevent security gaps. Organizations must establish policies that define how these identities are created, authenticated, and deactivated to maintain a secure identity lifecycle.

APIs play a significant role in modern IT ecosystems, enabling applications and services to exchange data and functionality. API keys and OAuth tokens are commonly used to authenticate API requests, but without proper governance, these credentials can become security liabilities. Expired or leaked API keys can be exploited by attackers to gain unauthorized access to cloud services, databases, and enterprise applications. Organizations should enforce API security best practices, including token expiration policies, access scopes, and encryption of sensitive credentials. API gateways and identity federation mechanisms further enhance security by centralizing authentication and access control for API-based interactions.

In cloud environments, managing service accounts and non-human identities presents additional challenges due to the dynamic nature of cloud workloads. Cloud service providers offer built-in identity and access management (IAM) solutions, such as AWS IAM roles, Google Cloud service accounts, and Azure Managed Identities, to facilitate secure authentication for cloud-based applications and services. These solutions eliminate the need for static credentials by providing temporary security tokens that automatically expire, reducing the risk of credential exposure. Organizations should leverage these native cloud IAM capabilities to enforce least privilege access and prevent unauthorized access to cloud resources.

Logging and monitoring service account activity is essential for detecting suspicious behavior and preventing unauthorized access. Unlike human users, service accounts typically exhibit predictable access patterns, making deviations from normal behavior potential indicators of compromise. Security information and event management (SIEM) solutions can analyze service account activities, flagging anomalies such as access attempts from unusual locations, excessive failed login attempts, or privilege escalation attempts. Integrating service account monitoring with behavioral analytics and AI-driven threat detection enhances an organization's ability to respond to security incidents in real time.

Automating the lifecycle management of service accounts is a key strategy for reducing security risks. Many organizations struggle with orphaned service accounts—accounts that remain active even after their associated applications or processes are no longer in use. Without proper governance, these orphaned accounts can become entry points for attackers. IAM solutions that support automated service account discovery, provisioning, and deprovisioning help organizations maintain visibility and control over their non-human identities. Automated access reviews and expiration policies further ensure that service accounts are regularly evaluated and removed when they are no longer needed.

Compliance requirements mandate strict control over service accounts and non-human identities to protect sensitive data and prevent unauthorized access. Regulations such as GDPR, HIPAA, PCI-DSS, and SOC 2 require organizations to enforce access controls, audit service account usage, and implement security measures to protect credentials. Organizations must maintain comprehensive audit logs detailing service account activities, including authentication attempts, privilege escalations, and data access events. Regular compliance audits and penetration testing help identify weaknesses in service account management practices and ensure adherence to regulatory standards.

Organizations adopting DevOps methodologies and infrastructure-as-code (IaC) must also integrate identity security into their development pipelines. DevOps environments rely heavily on automation, using service accounts and non-human identities to deploy code, manage cloud resources, and orchestrate infrastructure. Security teams should embed identity governance into DevOps workflows, ensuring that service accounts follow security best practices from creation to decommissioning. Policy-as-code frameworks allow organizations to enforce identity security policies programmatically, reducing the risk of misconfigurations and unauthorized access.

As organizations continue to expand their use of automation, cloud services, and machine identities, securing service accounts and non-human identities will remain a critical priority. By implementing strong authentication mechanisms, enforcing least privilege access, automating credential management, and continuously monitoring identity activity, organizations can reduce the risks associated with non-human identities while maintaining operational efficiency. A proactive approach to identity security ensures that service accounts and non-human identities are governed effectively, minimizing the attack surface and protecting enterprise systems from evolving cybersecurity threats.

Identity Lifecycle in Hybrid IT Environments

Managing the identity lifecycle in hybrid IT environments presents unique challenges as organizations operate across both on-premises and cloud-based infrastructures. Hybrid IT environments combine legacy systems, private data centers, cloud applications, and remote workforce technologies, creating a complex landscape for identity and access management (IAM). Ensuring seamless identity lifecycle management across these environments requires a unified strategy that integrates identity provisioning, authentication, access control, and deprovisioning while maintaining security, compliance, and operational efficiency.

Identity provisioning in hybrid environments involves creating user accounts across multiple systems and platforms while ensuring consistency and security. When a new employee, contractor, or partner joins an organization, their identity must be established in both on-premises directories, such as Microsoft Active Directory (AD), and cloud-based identity providers, such as Azure Active Directory (Azure AD), Okta, or Google Workspace. Automated identity synchronization between on-premises and cloud systems ensures that users have seamless access to enterprise applications while maintaining centralized control over identity management. Without proper synchronization, inconsistencies in identity attributes can lead to authentication failures, duplicate accounts, or security gaps.

Authentication and access control are critical components of managing identities in hybrid IT environments. Traditional authentication methods relying solely on passwords are insufficient for securing access across distributed systems. Organizations implement multi-factor authentication (MFA) to enhance security, requiring additional verification beyond passwords to protect against credential-based attacks. Adaptive authentication further improves security by analyzing risk signals, such as login locations, device health, and behavioral patterns, to determine whether additional authentication steps are necessary.

Federated identity management enables users to authenticate once and access multiple applications across hybrid environments without managing separate credentials. Organizations leverage identity federation protocols such as Security Assertion Markup Language (SAML), OpenID Connect (OIDC), and OAuth 2.0 to establish trust between on-premises identity providers and cloud applications. Single Sign-On (SSO) solutions further streamline authentication by allowing users to access enterprise resources with a single set of credentials, reducing login friction and improving security posture.

Managing access control in hybrid environments requires a combination of role-based access control (RBAC) and attribute-based access control (ABAC). RBAC assigns permissions based on predefined roles, ensuring that users receive appropriate access based on their job functions. ABAC enhances access control by evaluating additional contextual attributes, such as department, location, device type, and security clearance, to determine access decisions dynamically. Hybrid environments benefit from a flexible access control approach that adapts to real-time business and security requirements.

The identity lifecycle extends beyond initial provisioning and authentication, requiring continuous access management as users transition within an organization. Employees frequently change roles, transfer departments, or take on new responsibilities, necessitating modifications to their access privileges. Without automated identity lifecycle management, users may accumulate excessive permissions over time, leading to privilege creep and security risks. Organizations implement access review processes and automated entitlement management to ensure that users retain only the necessary access required for their roles.

Managing privileged access in hybrid IT environments introduces additional security challenges, as administrative accounts often have elevated permissions across on-premises infrastructure, cloud services, and remote management tools. Privileged access management (PAM) solutions enforce strict access controls by securing administrator credentials, implementing session monitoring, and enforcing just-in-time (JIT) access provisioning. Cloud-based PAM solutions integrate with hybrid IAM frameworks to extend privileged access security across distributed environments while maintaining centralized governance.

Identity governance and compliance play a critical role in managing identities across hybrid IT environments. Organizations must adhere to industry regulations such as GDPR, HIPAA, SOX, and NIST, requiring strict controls over identity lifecycle management, access reviews, and audit logging. Compliance mandates require organizations to maintain visibility into user access, enforce segregation of duties (SoD), and document identity lifecycle activities to prevent unauthorized access and data breaches. Identity governance solutions provide reporting and monitoring capabilities that enable organizations to track access events, detect anomalies, and generate compliance audit reports.

User deprovisioning in hybrid environments must be handled with precision to prevent security risks associated with orphaned accounts. When an employee leaves an organization or a contractor's engagement ends, their access must be revoked across all on-premises and cloud systems simultaneously. Delays in deprovisioning can result in lingering access to critical applications, increasing the risk of insider threats and credential misuse. Automated deprovisioning workflows integrated with HR systems and identity providers ensure that user accounts are promptly disabled, reducing the likelihood of unauthorized access.

Hybrid IT environments also introduce challenges related to machine identities, service accounts, and non-human identities. Automated workloads, API-driven integrations, and cloud-native applications require authentication mechanisms to access enterprise resources securely. Managing the lifecycle of non-human identities involves securing API keys, rotating credentials, and implementing strict access controls to prevent misuse. Organizations leverage identity federation and cloud-native IAM services to extend identity governance to machine identities while maintaining visibility and control.

Security monitoring and anomaly detection are essential for identifying identity-related threats in hybrid environments.

Organizations deploy security information and event management (SIEM) solutions to analyze authentication logs, access patterns, and privileged account activities. AI-driven identity analytics enhance security by detecting unusual behaviors, such as login attempts from unrecognized locations or privilege escalation attempts. Integrating SIEM with IAM solutions enables real-time threat detection and automated response to identity-related security incidents.

Cloud access security brokers (CASBs) play a crucial role in enforcing identity policies across hybrid environments. CASBs provide visibility into cloud application usage, enforce data loss prevention (DLP) policies, and monitor risky access behaviors. By integrating CASBs with identity lifecycle management, organizations can extend security controls to cloud services, ensuring that user identities are managed consistently across hybrid infrastructures.

As organizations expand their digital ecosystems, effective identity lifecycle management in hybrid IT environments becomes essential for maintaining security, compliance, and operational efficiency. Organizations must adopt automated identity workflows, enforce strong authentication measures, and continuously monitor access activities to mitigate risks associated with hybrid identity management. A unified approach to identity lifecycle management ensures that user identities remain secure, properly governed, and seamlessly integrated across both on-premises and cloud-based environments.

Compliance and Regulatory Requirements in Identity Management

Compliance and regulatory requirements play a crucial role in identity management, ensuring that organizations implement proper controls to protect user identities, sensitive data, and access privileges. As cyber threats continue to evolve, regulatory bodies worldwide enforce strict identity management policies to reduce security risks, prevent fraud, and maintain data privacy. Organizations must align their identity and access management (IAM) strategies with compliance frameworks to avoid legal penalties, reputational damage, and operational disruptions. Adhering to regulatory requirements requires a combination of strong authentication, access controls, audit capabilities, and identity governance practices.

Regulations such as the General Data Protection Regulation (GDPR) in Europe, the Health Insurance Portability and Accountability Act (HIPAA) in the United States, the Sarbanes-Oxley Act (SOX), and the Payment Card Industry Data Security Standard (PCI-DSS) mandate strict identity security measures. Each regulation imposes specific identity management requirements based on industry needs. GDPR focuses on protecting personal data by enforcing access controls, encryption, and user consent mechanisms. HIPAA requires healthcare organizations to implement role-based access control (RBAC) to restrict access to electronic health records (EHRs) and ensure only authorized personnel can view sensitive patient data. SOX mandates that financial institutions enforce strong identity governance by auditing user access to prevent fraudulent activities. PCI-DSS applies to organizations handling payment transactions, requiring strict authentication measures to protect cardholder data from unauthorized access.

One of the primary identity management requirements in compliance frameworks is access control. Organizations must implement the principle of least privilege (PoLP), ensuring that users receive only the minimum access necessary to perform their job functions. Role-based access control (RBAC) and attribute-based access control (ABAC) help enforce access policies by granting permissions based on user attributes, roles, and security clearance. Regulatory compliance requires organizations to continuously review and adjust access rights to prevent privilege creep, where users accumulate excessive permissions over time.

Multi-factor authentication (MFA) is a critical requirement in many compliance frameworks, adding an extra layer of security to prevent unauthorized access. Regulations such as PCI-DSS and NIST 800-63B mandate the use of MFA for accessing sensitive systems and data. Organizations implement MFA by requiring users to verify their identity through multiple authentication factors, such as passwords, biometric verification, or hardware tokens. Adaptive authentication further enhances security by assessing risk factors, such as login location and device health, before granting access.

Identity governance and administration (IGA) ensure compliance by providing visibility into user access, enforcing security policies, and automating identity lifecycle management. Regulatory frameworks require organizations to conduct regular access reviews, ensuring that users maintain appropriate permissions and that outdated or unnecessary access rights are revoked. Automated access certification processes help organizations streamline compliance audits by providing reports on user entitlements, policy violations, and access history.

Auditing and reporting are essential components of compliance in identity management. Regulations such as SOX and GDPR require organizations to maintain detailed logs of identity-related activities, including user authentication attempts, privilege escalations, and access modifications. Security information and event management (SIEM) solutions integrate with IAM platforms to generate real-time audit logs, enabling organizations to detect and investigate suspicious access events. Compliance audits assess whether identity management policies align with regulatory standards, identifying gaps and recommending corrective actions.

Data protection regulations emphasize the need for identity-centric security measures to prevent unauthorized data access and breaches. GDPR mandates strict data access controls, requiring organizations to implement encryption, anonymization, and pseudonymization techniques to protect personally identifiable information (PII). Identity-based data access policies ensure that only authorized users can retrieve, modify, or share sensitive data. Data loss prevention (DLP) solutions further enhance compliance by monitoring and restricting unauthorized data transfers, preventing data exposure through email, cloud storage, and external devices.

Identity lifecycle management plays a vital role in regulatory compliance, ensuring that user identities are properly created, modified, and deprovisioned throughout their tenure in an organization. Compliance frameworks require organizations to implement automated identity provisioning processes that integrate with human resources (HR) systems, reducing the risk of orphaned accounts—active accounts belonging to former employees or contractors. Deprovisioning processes must revoke access immediately when a user leaves the organization or changes roles, preventing unauthorized access to corporate systems.

Privileged access management (PAM) is a key compliance requirement for securing administrative accounts, which have elevated permissions that could be exploited in cyberattacks. Regulations such as SOX and PCI-DSS mandate strict controls over privileged accounts, requiring organizations to implement just-in-time (JIT) access provisioning, session monitoring, and privileged access auditing. PAM solutions enforce password vaulting, ensuring that privileged credentials are securely stored, rotated regularly, and not shared among multiple users.

Cloud identity management presents additional compliance challenges, as organizations must secure access to cloud applications, hybrid environments, and third-party integrations. Regulations such as the California Consumer Privacy Act (CCPA) and the ISO 27001 standard emphasize the need for strong cloud access controls, requiring organizations to implement federated identity management, single sign-on (SSO), and API security measures. Compliance with cloud security standards ensures that user identities are protected across distributed IT infrastructures, reducing the risk of unauthorized access and data breaches.

Regulatory frameworks continue to evolve as cyber threats and data privacy concerns increase. Governments and industry bodies introduce new compliance requirements to address emerging security risks, such as identity fraud, insider threats, and biometric data protection. Organizations must stay informed about regulatory changes, adapting their identity management strategies to align with new security mandates. Continuous compliance monitoring, policy enforcement, and security awareness training help organizations maintain compliance while strengthening their overall cybersecurity posture.

By implementing IAM best practices, enforcing strong authentication measures, and automating compliance workflows, organizations can meet regulatory requirements while enhancing identity security. A proactive approach to compliance in identity management reduces risks, protects sensitive data, and ensures that access to enterprise resources remains secure and well-governed.

Identity Audits and Reporting

Identity audits and reporting are critical components of identity and access management (IAM), ensuring that organizations maintain visibility and control over user identities, access permissions, and security policies. As businesses expand their digital footprint across cloud environments, enterprise applications, and hybrid IT infrastructures, the need for regular identity audits has become more important than ever. Auditing user identities and access rights helps organizations detect unauthorized access, enforce least privilege principles, comply with regulatory requirements, and mitigate security risks associated with identity misuse.

An identity audit involves systematically reviewing user accounts, roles, and permissions to verify that access privileges align with business needs and security policies. Organizations conduct identity audits to ensure that users do not retain excessive or outdated permissions, reducing the risk of privilege creep and insider threats. By regularly assessing identity data, businesses can identify discrepancies, orphaned accounts, and unauthorized entitlements before they lead to security incidents. Identity audits help enforce access governance by validating that only authorized users can access sensitive systems and information.

Access reviews are an essential part of identity audits, requiring managers, system owners, and compliance teams to evaluate and certify user permissions. Periodic access reviews ensure that employees, contractors, and third-party users maintain appropriate access levels and that unnecessary privileges are revoked. Automated access review processes streamline audit workflows by generating reports, notifying reviewers, and enforcing corrective actions based on approval or revocation decisions. Organizations that fail to conduct regular access reviews risk accumulating excessive permissions, which can be exploited by attackers to gain unauthorized access.

Audit logs play a crucial role in identity reporting by providing a comprehensive record of authentication attempts, access requests, privilege escalations, and user activity. Logging identity-related events enables organizations to track how identities are used, detect anomalies, and investigate suspicious behavior. Security information and event management (SIEM) solutions integrate with IAM systems to collect and analyze identity logs, helping security teams identify unauthorized access patterns, detect potential breaches, and respond to threats in real time.

Identity reporting provides organizations with actionable insights into identity management activities, user access trends, and security compliance. Reports generated from identity audits highlight areas of risk, such as inactive accounts, excessive permissions, and failed authentication attempts. Compliance-focused reports demonstrate adherence to regulatory requirements, such as GDPR, HIPAA, and SOX, by documenting user access certifications, policy enforcement actions, and identity governance activities. Identity reporting dashboards offer real-time visibility into access controls, helping organizations make informed decisions about security and compliance strategies.

Privileged account audits are essential for securing administrative access to critical systems and applications. Privileged accounts, such as system administrators, domain controllers, and cloud service administrators, have elevated permissions that, if misused or compromised, could lead to significant security breaches. Organizations conduct privileged access audits to verify that administrator accounts are properly managed, protected, and monitored. Privileged access management (PAM) solutions enforce security policies by restricting access to privileged accounts, implementing session monitoring, and requiring multi-factor authentication (MFA) for high-risk actions.

Identity reconciliation audits ensure that user identities remain consistent across multiple directories, applications, and identity providers. As organizations operate in hybrid IT environments, identity data often resides in different systems, leading to inconsistencies and potential security gaps. Identity reconciliation audits compare user attributes, group memberships, and entitlements across identity repositories, identifying discrepancies that require remediation. Automated identity synchronization solutions help maintain accurate identity records by updating attributes and access rights in real time.

Orphaned account detection is a key objective of identity audits, as inactive or unmonitored accounts pose a significant security risk. Orphaned accounts occur when employees leave an organization, but their access credentials remain active due to incomplete deprovisioning processes. Attackers often target orphaned accounts to gain unauthorized access to corporate systems without triggering security alerts. Regular audits identify and disable orphaned accounts, ensuring that former employees, contractors, and vendors do not retain access to enterprise resources.

Audit trails provide a historical record of identity-related changes, access approvals, and authentication events, supporting forensic investigations and compliance audits. In the event of a security breach or policy violation, organizations rely on audit trails to trace unauthorized activities, identify responsible users, and implement corrective measures. Well-documented audit trails strengthen security posture by increasing accountability, enabling security teams to reconstruct events and take proactive steps to prevent future incidents.

Identity audits also assess compliance with industry regulations and internal security policies. Regulatory frameworks require organizations to maintain strict controls over user access, enforce segregation of duties (SoD), and document identity governance activities. Auditors review identity management processes to verify compliance with legal requirements and corporate policies. Non-compliance can result in financial penalties, reputational damage, and increased risk exposure. Automated compliance reporting simplifies audit preparation by generating detailed reports that demonstrate regulatory adherence and access control enforcement.

Risk-based identity audits leverage artificial intelligence and machine learning to identify high-risk users, anomalous behavior, and access violations. AI-driven identity analytics analyze login patterns, privilege assignments, and authentication failures to detect insider threats and potential security breaches. By prioritizing audit findings based on risk severity, organizations can focus on addressing the most critical identity-related vulnerabilities. Risk-based identity audits enhance security operations by enabling proactive threat detection and mitigation.

Role-based access audits validate that users are assigned appropriate roles based on job functions and responsibilities. Organizations using role-based access control (RBAC) must ensure that role assignments align with business needs and security policies. Role mining techniques analyze user behavior and access patterns to identify inconsistencies in role assignments, suggesting optimizations to reduce over-permissioning. Organizations that implement regular role-based access audits maintain better control over access entitlements, reducing the likelihood of excessive or misconfigured permissions.

Real-time identity monitoring supplements periodic audits by continuously tracking identity-related activities and generating alerts for security incidents. Continuous monitoring detects suspicious login attempts, unauthorized privilege escalations, and deviations from normal user behavior. Organizations integrate identity monitoring with automated response mechanisms, enabling security teams to investigate and remediate access anomalies before they escalate into security breaches.

Identity audits and reporting enable organizations to maintain security, enforce compliance, and improve identity governance. By implementing automated access reviews, logging identity events, and leveraging AI-driven risk analysis, businesses can proactively manage user identities, detect security threats, and align with regulatory standards. Regular audits and comprehensive reporting strengthen identity management practices, ensuring that organizations maintain a secure and well-governed identity ecosystem.

Risk-Based Access and Adaptive Authentication

Risk-based access and adaptive authentication are essential components of modern identity and access management (IAM), ensuring that authentication and authorization decisions are made based on real-time risk assessments. Traditional access control models rely on static rules, such as passwords and predefined roles, which do not account for evolving security threats, dynamic user behaviors, or contextual risk factors. Risk-based access and adaptive authentication enhance security by analyzing contextual signals and dynamically adjusting authentication requirements based on the level of risk associated with an access attempt.

Risk-based access evaluates various risk factors before granting or denying access to a system or resource. These factors include user behavior, device type, geographic location, network security posture, and access history. If an authentication attempt exhibits characteristics that deviate from a user's normal behavior, the system may prompt for additional verification, restrict access, or deny the request altogether. This dynamic approach reduces the likelihood of credential theft, account takeovers, and unauthorized access while minimizing friction for legitimate users.

Adaptive authentication builds upon risk-based access by applying real-time intelligence to authentication workflows. Instead of enforcing a one-size-fits-all security policy, adaptive authentication dynamically adjusts authentication requirements based on risk analysis. If a user logs in from a trusted device and location, they may be allowed access with minimal authentication steps. However, if the same user attempts to access an account from an unrecognized device, unusual location, or high-risk network, the system may require multi-factor authentication (MFA), biometric verification, or additional security checks before granting access.

One of the primary advantages of risk-based access and adaptive authentication is the ability to enhance security without introducing unnecessary friction for users. Traditional security models often impose strict authentication requirements on all users, regardless of risk levels. This approach can lead to poor user experience, increased password fatigue, and higher support costs due to frequent password resets. By leveraging adaptive authentication, organizations can balance security with usability, ensuring that legitimate users can access resources smoothly while blocking suspicious or high-risk attempts.

Risk signals used in adaptive authentication are collected from multiple data sources and analyzed using machine learning and artificial intelligence (AI). These signals include login frequency, IP reputation, device fingerprinting, browser type, and behavioral analytics. AI-driven authentication systems continuously learn from user behavior patterns, detecting anomalies that indicate potential threats. If a login attempt appears suspicious, AI models can trigger step-up authentication, requiring the user to provide additional credentials, such as a one-time password (OTP) or biometric verification.

Geolocation and network security are critical factors in risk-based access decisions. If a user attempts to access a corporate system from a known location, such as their office or home network, the system may classify the attempt as low risk and allow access with minimal authentication. However, if the same user attempts to log in from a country where they have never traveled before, the system may flag the request as high risk and require additional verification steps. Organizations can also integrate risk-based access controls with security policies that block access from certain high-risk regions, mitigating the risk of credential theft from foreign cybercriminals.

Device trust assessment plays a significant role in adaptive authentication. Organizations track whether a device has been previously registered or if it meets security compliance standards. Trusted devices that meet security requirements, such as up-to-date operating systems, endpoint protection software, and encrypted storage, may be granted access without additional authentication. In contrast, untrusted or compromised devices may require extra verification or be denied access altogether. This approach strengthens security by ensuring that only secure endpoints are allowed to connect to enterprise resources.

Behavioral biometrics further enhance risk-based access by analyzing user behavior patterns, such as typing speed, mouse movement, and navigation habits. If an authentication attempt exhibits behavior that significantly deviates from a user's established patterns, the system may suspect fraud and initiate additional security checks. Behavioral analytics help detect sophisticated threats, such as session hijacking and credential stuffing, by identifying anomalies that traditional authentication methods might miss.

Risk-based access is particularly valuable in securing privileged accounts, which are prime targets for cybercriminals. Privileged users, such as system administrators and executives, often have access to highly sensitive data and critical infrastructure. Organizations implement risk-based access controls to continuously monitor privileged account activity, detecting unusual login attempts, excessive access requests, or unauthorized privilege escalations. If a privileged user's behavior deviates from normal patterns, automated risk-based policies can trigger alerts, restrict access, or require additional approvals before executing high-risk actions.

Cloud-based IAM solutions integrate risk-based access and adaptive authentication to secure cloud applications, remote work environments, and multi-cloud ecosystems. Organizations adopting hybrid IT infrastructures leverage risk-aware access policies to enforce dynamic security controls across both on-premises and cloud environments. Cloud access security brokers (CASBs) enhance these capabilities by enforcing adaptive authentication policies for cloud-based applications, ensuring that access decisions are based on real-time risk assessments.

Regulatory compliance mandates the use of risk-based authentication for protecting sensitive data and ensuring secure access. Standards such as GDPR, HIPAA, PCI-DSS, and NIST 800-63B require organizations to implement strong authentication controls based on risk assessments. Compliance-driven identity governance frameworks incorporate risk-based access policies to enforce access reviews, audit user activities, and ensure that only authorized individuals can access regulated data. Automated compliance reporting further helps organizations demonstrate adherence to security standards by providing detailed records of authentication events, risk evaluations, and policy enforcement actions.

Implementing risk-based access and adaptive authentication requires organizations to integrate IAM solutions with security analytics platforms, threat intelligence feeds, and behavioral analysis engines. Security orchestration and automation tools enhance adaptive authentication by dynamically adjusting security policies based on evolving threat landscapes. Organizations that leverage real-time risk assessments and AI-driven authentication models gain a proactive security advantage, reducing the likelihood of identity-based attacks while providing a seamless user experience.

Risk-based access and adaptive authentication continue to evolve as cybersecurity threats become more sophisticated. Organizations adopting zero trust security models integrate these technologies to enforce continuous authentication, verify user identities dynamically, and prevent unauthorized access based on contextual risk analysis. By implementing intelligent access controls, organizations enhance security resilience, protect sensitive data, and improve authentication processes in an increasingly complex digital landscape.

The Role of Artificial Intelligence in Identity Management

Artificial intelligence (AI) is transforming identity management by enhancing security, automating processes, and improving the accuracy of access controls. Traditional identity and access management (IAM) systems rely on predefined rules, static policies, and manual oversight to manage user identities, permissions, and authentication. However, as cyber threats evolve and IT environments become more complex, AI-driven identity management solutions provide a more adaptive, intelligent, and scalable approach to securing digital identities. By leveraging machine learning, behavioral analytics, and automation, AI enhances identity governance, strengthens authentication mechanisms, and reduces security risks.

AI plays a crucial role in identity verification by improving the accuracy of identity proofing and fraud detection. Traditional identity verification methods, such as knowledge-based authentication (KBA) and document-based validation, are increasingly vulnerable to social engineering attacks, credential theft, and identity fraud. AI-powered identity verification solutions analyze multiple data points, including biometric patterns, device reputation, and historical user behavior, to confirm an individual's identity with higher accuracy. Facial recognition, fingerprint scanning, and voice authentication leverage AI algorithms to detect anomalies and prevent fraudulent attempts to impersonate legitimate users.

Behavioral biometrics further enhance identity management by continuously monitoring user interactions to detect unauthorized access. Unlike traditional authentication methods that rely on passwords or one-time authentication codes, behavioral biometrics analyze how users type, move their mouse, swipe on mobile devices, and interact with applications. AI models learn these behavioral patterns and create user profiles that serve as a second layer of authentication. If an access attempt deviates from an established behavioral profile, the system can trigger additional authentication steps or block access. This approach significantly reduces the risk of account takeovers and credential-based attacks.

AI-driven access control enables organizations to implement adaptive security measures that respond to real-time risk assessments. Traditional access control models, such as role-based access control (RBAC) and attribute-based access control (ABAC), assign permissions based on predefined policies that may not account for evolving threats. AI enhances these models by analyzing contextual signals, such as user behavior, geolocation, device health, and network security posture, to determine the appropriate level of access dynamically. Instead of granting static permissions, AI-driven systems adjust access rights based on real-time risk evaluations, reducing over-permissioning and preventing unauthorized access.

Identity lifecycle management benefits from AI-driven automation, improving efficiency and reducing the administrative burden associated with user provisioning, access reviews, and deprovisioning. Traditional IAM processes require IT teams to manually create, modify, and revoke user accounts based on job changes, contract terminations, and organizational restructuring. AI automates these processes by detecting anomalies in user behavior, identifying inactive accounts, and recommending access changes based on predictive analytics. Automated identity governance ensures that access rights remain aligned with business needs while minimizing human errors and security gaps.

AI enhances privileged access management (PAM) by monitoring and securing high-risk accounts that have elevated permissions. Privileged accounts, such as system administrators and cloud service managers, are prime targets for cyberattacks due to their ability to execute critical system changes. AI-powered PAM solutions analyze privileged account behavior, detect deviations from normal usage patterns, and flag suspicious activities for immediate investigation. If a privileged user attempts to access sensitive data from an unfamiliar location or escalates privileges unexpectedly, AI-driven security controls can automatically initiate alerts, enforce step-up authentication, or terminate the session to prevent potential breaches.

Anomaly detection and threat intelligence are core functions of AI in identity management. Cybercriminals continuously develop new tactics to bypass traditional security measures, making it difficult for static rule-based systems to detect emerging threats. AI models continuously learn from historical identity-related data, identifying patterns that indicate credential stuffing, phishing attacks, and unauthorized access attempts. AI-driven threat detection systems analyze authentication logs, failed login attempts, and access request patterns to detect anomalies and prevent security breaches before they escalate.

Real-time identity monitoring is another critical application of AI in identity management. Organizations with large workforces, remote employees, and hybrid IT environments struggle to track user activity across multiple systems and applications. AI-powered identity analytics platforms continuously monitor user access, detect policy violations, and provide actionable insights into security risks. By analyzing vast amounts of identity data, AI helps security teams prioritize high-risk incidents, reduce false positives, and respond to threats more effectively.

AI-powered chatbots and virtual assistants streamline identity-related support tasks, reducing the workload on IT helpdesks. Users frequently require assistance with password resets, account unlocks, and access requests, leading to increased operational costs and delays. AI-driven chatbots integrate with IAM platforms to provide automated self-service solutions, guiding users through authentication steps, verifying identities, and executing routine access management tasks. By leveraging natural language processing (NLP) and machine learning, AI-driven support systems enhance user experience while improving security and efficiency.

Cloud identity management benefits significantly from AI, as organizations adopt multi-cloud and hybrid cloud environments that require consistent access controls across different platforms. AI-driven

IAM solutions integrate with cloud identity providers, such as Azure AD, Okta, and Google Cloud Identity, to enforce security policies, detect access anomalies, and prevent unauthorized access to cloud applications. AI also helps organizations enforce Zero Trust principles by continuously verifying user identities, assessing risk levels, and adapting security controls based on changing threat conditions.

Regulatory compliance and audit reporting are enhanced by AI-driven identity governance solutions. Compliance frameworks such as GDPR, HIPAA, and SOX require organizations to enforce strict identity controls, conduct access reviews, and maintain audit logs for regulatory inspections. AI automates compliance reporting by generating audit trails, detecting policy violations, and ensuring that identity management practices align with regulatory requirements. By reducing manual compliance tasks, AI enables organizations to improve security while meeting industry standards more efficiently.

Organizations adopting AI-driven identity management must ensure that AI models are transparent, unbiased, and aligned with ethical considerations. AI systems that process identity data and authentication requests must be designed to prevent discrimination, bias, and privacy violations. Organizations should implement governance frameworks that define AI usage policies, conduct regular audits of AI-driven IAM solutions, and ensure compliance with data protection regulations. By incorporating ethical AI principles, organizations can enhance trust in identity management systems while mitigating potential risks associated with AI decision-making.

AI continues to reshape identity management by introducing advanced automation, predictive analytics, and real-time threat detection capabilities. As cyber threats grow in complexity, AI-driven identity solutions provide a proactive approach to securing digital identities, reducing administrative overhead, and enhancing authentication processes. Organizations that leverage AI-powered IAM technologies gain a competitive advantage in protecting sensitive data, preventing unauthorized access, and maintaining robust security postures in an increasingly digital world.

Automating Identity Workflows

Automating identity workflows is a key strategy for improving efficiency, security, and compliance in identity and access management (IAM). As organizations expand their IT environments across on-premises systems, cloud applications, and hybrid infrastructures, managing user identities manually becomes increasingly complex and prone to errors. Automating identity-related processes ensures that user accounts are created, modified, and revoked in a timely manner while reducing administrative overhead and mitigating security risks associated with human intervention. By leveraging automation, organizations can enforce access policies, streamline onboarding and offboarding, and improve identity governance.

User provisioning is one of the most critical identity workflows that benefits from automation. When a new employee, contractor, or third-party vendor joins an organization, their identity must be established, and appropriate access must be granted to the necessary systems and applications. Traditional manual provisioning processes require IT administrators to create accounts, assign permissions, and configure access settings, which can lead to delays and inconsistencies. Automated provisioning integrates IAM platforms with human resources (HR) systems, ensuring that user identities are created as soon as an employment record is generated. Role-based access control (RBAC) and attribute-based access control (ABAC) models further enhance automation by assigning access based on predefined policies, reducing the risk of over-provisioning and unauthorized access.

Identity lifecycle management extends beyond initial provisioning to include access modifications as users change roles, departments, or responsibilities. Without automation, organizations struggle to keep up with role transitions, leading to privilege creep—where users accumulate unnecessary permissions over time. Automated identity workflows track changes in HR systems, dynamically adjusting access rights based on job function updates. If an employee is promoted, their access is automatically modified to align with their new role, while any permissions associated with their previous position are revoked. This automated process ensures that users only retain the necessary access required for their current responsibilities, enforcing the principle of least privilege.

Automated deprovisioning is essential for maintaining security when users leave an organization or complete temporary assignments. Orphaned accounts—accounts that remain active after a user's departure—pose a significant security risk, as attackers can exploit them to gain unauthorized access to corporate systems. Automating the deprovisioning process ensures that user accounts, credentials, and permissions are revoked immediately when an employment status changes in the HR system. Additionally, automation enables organizations to enforce staged deprovisioning, where access to critical systems is removed first while retaining minimal access for a transition period, preventing operational disruptions.

Multi-factor authentication (MFA) and adaptive authentication workflows can also be automated to enhance security. Instead of applying static authentication policies to all users, organizations use automation to enforce dynamic authentication based on risk levels. If a user attempts to log in from an unfamiliar device or geographic location, automated workflows trigger step-up authentication, requiring additional verification before granting access. Risk-based authentication powered by artificial intelligence (AI) continuously monitors user behavior, detecting anomalies and adjusting authentication requirements accordingly. By automating these workflows, organizations strengthen security without adding unnecessary friction to the user experience.

Access request management is another area where automation improves efficiency. Employees and contractors frequently need access to specific applications, data, or systems based on project requirements or temporary job functions. Manual access request processes often involve multiple approval steps, resulting in delays and administrative burden. Automated access request workflows enable users to request access through self-service portals, where predefined approval rules determine whether requests are granted or escalated for review. Integrating identity governance solutions ensures that approvals align with security policies and compliance regulations, preventing unauthorized access while streamlining the approval process.

Automating identity audits and compliance reporting helps organizations meet regulatory requirements while reducing the workload on IT and security teams. Regulations such as GDPR, HIPAA, and SOX mandate strict controls over user identities, requiring organizations to conduct periodic access reviews and generate audit reports. Automated identity governance platforms continuously monitor access entitlements, flagging policy violations and generating compliance reports in real-time. Access review campaigns can be scheduled and executed automatically, sending notifications to managers and system owners to review user permissions and certify access rights. By automating these processes, organizations maintain compliance while minimizing human error and audit preparation time.

Privileged access management (PAM) benefits significantly from automation, as privileged accounts require strict security controls to prevent unauthorized access. Instead of relying on manual processes to grant and revoke privileged access, organizations implement just-in-time (JIT) access workflows, where users receive temporary administrative privileges only when needed. Automated session monitoring captures privileged activities in real-time, flagging suspicious behavior and enforcing security policies. Privileged credentials are rotated automatically, preventing attackers from exploiting static administrator passwords. By integrating PAM automation with IAM solutions, organizations enhance security while maintaining operational flexibility.

Identity synchronization across multiple systems and platforms is another crucial function that automation improves. Many organizations operate in hybrid IT environments where identity data is stored in on-premises directories, cloud identity providers, and third-party applications. Automated identity synchronization ensures that changes made in one system are propagated across all connected platforms, maintaining consistency and reducing administrative workload. If a user updates their profile information, automation ensures that the changes reflect in all integrated systems without requiring manual intervention. Synchronization also extends to API-based identity management, where applications exchange identity data securely and efficiently through automated workflows.

AI-driven identity automation enhances IAM processes by leveraging machine learning algorithms to detect patterns, predict security risks, and recommend access optimizations. AI-powered identity analytics analyze user behavior, detecting anomalies that indicate potential security threats, such as unauthorized privilege escalations or unusual access requests. Automation enables organizations to respond to these threats in real-time, revoking risky access, enforcing additional authentication, or flagging accounts for manual review. As identity threats evolve, AI-driven automation ensures that identity workflows remain adaptive and proactive in mitigating security risks.

Organizations implementing automated identity workflows must also establish governance controls to ensure that automation aligns with business policies and security requirements. Automated workflows should be regularly reviewed and updated to accommodate changing regulations, organizational structures, and security policies. IAM platforms provide audit trails and monitoring capabilities that allow organizations to track automated actions, ensuring accountability and compliance. By combining automation with governance frameworks, organizations maintain a balance between efficiency, security, and regulatory adherence.

Automating identity workflows improves security, reduces administrative complexity, and enhances the user experience by ensuring seamless access management. By leveraging automation in provisioning, deprovisioning, access governance, authentication, and privileged access management, organizations create a more resilient identity management framework. As identity management continues to evolve, automation remains a key enabler in securing digital identities while supporting business agility and compliance requirements.

Identity Lifecycle and Zero Trust Security

The identity lifecycle and Zero Trust security model are closely intertwined, ensuring that user identities are continuously verified, managed, and secured throughout their existence in an organization's IT environment. Traditional security models operated on the assumption that once users were authenticated inside a corporate network, they could be trusted. However, the rise of cyber threats, remote work, cloud applications, and insider risks has rendered this approach ineffective. The Zero Trust model shifts the focus from perimeter-based security to identity-centric security, where every access request is evaluated dynamically based on context, behavior, and risk level. Managing identity lifecycles within a Zero Trust framework ensures that users receive the right access at the right time while minimizing security vulnerabilities.

The identity lifecycle begins with user onboarding, a critical phase where identities are created, provisioned, and authenticated before gaining access to corporate systems. In a Zero Trust architecture, onboarding requires strict identity verification to ensure that only legitimate users are granted accounts. Identity proofing techniques, such as biometric authentication, document verification, and multi-factor authentication (MFA), enhance security by reducing the risk of identity fraud. Automated identity provisioning solutions integrate with human resources (HR) systems to synchronize user data, ensuring that access is granted based on predefined roles, attributes, and policies. Unlike traditional access models that grant broad permissions, Zero Trust enforces least privilege access from the start, ensuring that new users only receive the minimum permissions necessary for their role.

Once users are onboarded, their identities must be continuously monitored and validated to maintain security and compliance. Zero Trust principles dictate that trust is never assumed, meaning that every access request is evaluated in real time. Continuous authentication techniques, such as risk-based authentication and behavioral biometrics, ensure that users remain verified throughout their sessions. If an identity exhibits unusual behavior, such as accessing resources from an unfamiliar location or attempting to escalate privileges, the system can trigger additional verification steps, restrict access, or terminate the session entirely. This dynamic approach prevents attackers from exploiting stolen credentials or compromised accounts.

Role transitions within an organization require ongoing identity lifecycle management to prevent privilege creep and unauthorized access. Employees frequently change positions, receive promotions, or switch departments, which necessitates modifying their access rights accordingly. In traditional identity management models, these changes often result in accumulated permissions that exceed what is necessary for the new role. Zero Trust enforces strict access governance, ensuring that old permissions are revoked when new permissions are assigned. Automated access reviews and identity governance solutions help enforce this policy by continuously auditing user entitlements and flagging excessive permissions for remediation.

Privileged access management (PAM) is a key component of Zero Trust security, ensuring that administrative accounts and high-risk users receive enhanced security controls. Privileged users, such as IT administrators, security analysts, and executives, often have access to critical systems that could be exploited if compromised. Zero Trust principles require that privileged access be granted on a just-in-time (JIT) basis, meaning that users receive elevated permissions only when needed and for a limited duration. Privileged session monitoring, keystroke logging, and access alerts help organizations detect and respond to suspicious activities in real time.

User deprovisioning is another essential phase of the identity lifecycle within a Zero Trust framework. When employees leave an organization, their access must be revoked immediately to prevent lingering permissions that could be exploited by insiders or external attackers. Traditional security models often result in orphaned accounts, where former employees retain active credentials that can be used maliciously. Zero Trust security automates deprovisioning by integrating with HR and IAM systems to disable accounts, revoke access, and remove digital certificates upon termination. Organizations enforce mandatory exit reviews to ensure that all access points, including cloud applications, remote desktops, and privileged accounts, are completely disabled.

Zero Trust security also extends to non-human identities, such as service accounts, application identities, and API keys. These identities are commonly used to automate processes, integrate systems, and enable cloud services. Without proper lifecycle management, service accounts can become security risks, as they are often overlooked in access reviews and lack monitoring mechanisms. Zero Trust mandates that machine identities follow the same security principles as human identities, requiring authentication, access controls, and regular audits. Automated secrets management and identity vaulting solutions secure non-human credentials by rotating API keys, restricting access to authorized applications, and logging usage for security monitoring.

Cloud identity management plays a crucial role in Zero Trust security, ensuring that identities are consistently secured across on-premises and cloud environments. Hybrid and multi-cloud architectures introduce additional complexity, as users access resources from various platforms and locations. Zero Trust enforces federated authentication, single sign-on (SSO), and identity federation to maintain consistent identity policies across different cloud providers. Organizations integrate Zero Trust principles with cloud-native IAM solutions, such as Azure AD, AWS IAM, and Google Cloud Identity, to enforce security policies, prevent unauthorized access, and monitor identity activities.

Continuous monitoring and threat detection are vital in Zero Trust identity lifecycle management. AI-driven identity analytics enhance security by analyzing user behavior, detecting anomalies, and predicting potential insider threats. Machine learning models evaluate authentication logs, access patterns, and privilege escalation attempts to identify suspicious activities before they result in a breach. Security information and event management (SIEM) solutions integrate with IAM platforms to provide real-time threat intelligence, enabling organizations to take proactive measures against identity-based threats.

Compliance and regulatory requirements align with Zero Trust identity lifecycle management by enforcing strict access controls, audit logging, and risk-based authentication. Regulations such as GDPR, HIPAA, and NIST mandate that organizations implement identity verification, least privilege access, and continuous monitoring to protect sensitive data. Zero Trust ensures compliance by automating identity governance, enforcing security policies, and maintaining detailed audit trails for regulatory reporting. Organizations that adopt Zero Trust identity management practices improve their ability to meet compliance requirements while reducing security risks.

As cyber threats evolve, identity lifecycle management within a Zero Trust framework becomes essential for maintaining security, efficiency, and regulatory adherence. By enforcing strict identity verification, continuous authentication, least privilege access, and automated deprovisioning, organizations can protect digital assets from unauthorized access and insider threats. Zero Trust transforms identity management into a proactive security strategy, ensuring that users, devices, and applications are continuously validated and monitored throughout their entire lifecycle.

Integrating Identity Management with HR Systems

Integrating identity management with human resources (HR) systems is a critical strategy for automating user lifecycle management, improving security, and ensuring compliance with access control policies. Organizations rely on HR systems as the source of truth for employee records, making them the ideal starting point for provisioning, updating, and deprovisioning user identities. By synchronizing HR data with identity and access management (IAM) solutions, businesses can enforce consistent access policies, reduce administrative overhead, and enhance security by preventing unauthorized access to corporate systems.

Identity lifecycle management begins with onboarding, where new employees, contractors, or temporary workers require access to enterprise applications, cloud services, and IT resources. Without HR system integration, user provisioning is often a manual and time-consuming process, requiring IT administrators to create accounts, assign roles, and configure permissions individually. Manual provisioning increases the risk of errors, leading to inconsistent access rights, privilege creep, or delays that impact productivity. By integrating IAM with HR systems, organizations automate provisioning workflows, ensuring that new users receive the correct access based on their role, department, and job function from day one.

Role-based access control (RBAC) and attribute-based access control (ABAC) play a crucial role in automated provisioning. HR systems store key identity attributes such as job title, location, department, and employment type, which IAM solutions use to define access policies. When a new hire is added to the HR system, identity management platforms automatically assign them predefined roles and permissions based on their job classification. This automated role assignment eliminates guesswork, ensures access consistency, and reduces the risk of over-provisioning, where users receive unnecessary or excessive permissions.

As employees progress through their careers, they often change roles, receive promotions, or transfer to different departments. Managing these transitions manually can lead to security gaps, as users may retain old permissions while gaining new ones, resulting in privilege creep. IAM integration with HR systems ensures that role transitions trigger automated access modifications. When an HR system updates an employee's role or department, identity management platforms adjust their access rights accordingly, revoking outdated permissions while granting new ones. This dynamic approach aligns access controls with business needs, reducing security risks associated with accumulated privileges.

HR system integration also enhances identity governance and compliance by automating access reviews and audits. Many regulatory frameworks, including GDPR, HIPAA, and SOX, require organizations to enforce strict access controls, conduct periodic access certifications, and maintain audit logs of identity-related activities. By linking HR data with IAM solutions, organizations can generate real-time reports on user access, detect policy violations, and streamline compliance audits. Automated access reviews allow managers to validate whether employees still require assigned permissions, ensuring that only authorized users retain access to critical systems.

Deprovisioning is one of the most critical identity management functions, preventing security risks associated with orphaned accounts. When employees leave an organization, their access must be revoked promptly to prevent unauthorized use of corporate resources. Without HR system integration, deprovisioning often relies on manual notifications, increasing the risk of delays or oversight. IAM solutions integrated with HR platforms automatically detect employment terminations, triggering immediate account deactivation, permission revocation, and session termination across all connected systems. This ensures that former employees cannot access sensitive data or enterprise applications after leaving the organization.

Contractor and temporary worker management benefits significantly from HR and IAM integration. Unlike permanent employees, contractors often have defined contract periods with specific access requirements. Organizations using manual identity management processes struggle to track and revoke contractor access, leading to unnecessary exposure of business systems. HR-integrated IAM platforms enforce time-based access policies, automatically disabling contractor accounts when their contract ends. Additionally, organizations can implement just-in-time (JIT) access provisioning for contractors, granting access only when needed and revoking it once tasks are completed.

Multi-factor authentication (MFA) policies can also be enhanced through HR-IAM integration. Certain job roles may require stricter authentication measures due to access to sensitive data or privileged accounts. By linking HR data with IAM platforms, organizations can enforce role-based MFA policies, ensuring that high-risk employees, such as administrators and finance personnel, authenticate using additional security factors. This dynamic authentication model strengthens security by applying risk-based authentication policies based on job responsibilities.

HR integration enables organizations to enforce security policies related to leave management and extended absences. Employees on long-term leave, sabbaticals, or parental leave may not require active access during their absence. Automated IAM workflows detect leave records in HR systems and temporarily suspend user access, preventing unnecessary exposure while allowing for easy reactivation upon return. This proactive security measure ensures that inactive accounts are not exploited by attackers while preserving user identity integrity.

Cloud-based HR platforms, such as Workday, SAP SuccessFactors, and Oracle HCM, have become standard for workforce management in modern enterprises. Integrating these cloud HR platforms with IAM solutions allows organizations to extend identity governance across hybrid and multi-cloud environments. Cloud-native IAM platforms support API-based integrations with HR systems, enabling real-time identity synchronization, automated access provisioning, and centralized user management. By leveraging cloud HR-IAM integration, organizations can streamline identity workflows across diverse IT landscapes without compromising security.

Artificial intelligence (AI) and machine learning (ML) further enhance HR-integrated identity management by detecting anomalies, predicting access risks, and optimizing identity governance policies. AI-driven IAM platforms analyze HR data, user behavior, and access patterns to identify unusual activities, such as unauthorized privilege escalations or excessive access requests. These insights help security teams proactively mitigate identity-based threats, refine access policies, and improve compliance enforcement.

Organizations implementing HR-IAM integration must also establish governance frameworks to manage identity synchronization effectively. Data consistency between HR and IAM platforms is crucial for maintaining accurate identity records and preventing conflicts. Identity validation rules, data normalization processes, and access approval workflows ensure that identity changes are processed accurately and securely. Additionally, organizations should implement identity reconciliation processes to detect discrepancies between HR and IAM records, resolving misconfigurations before they impact access control policies.

Integrating identity management with HR systems transforms IAM from a reactive security function into a proactive, automated identity governance strategy. By leveraging HR data for provisioning, access control, and deprovisioning, organizations enhance security, reduce administrative burden, and improve compliance with regulatory requirements. The combination of automated identity workflows, AI-driven security analytics, and cloud-based integrations ensures that HR-IAM synchronization remains an essential foundation for modern identity management practices.

Password Management and Self-Service Capabilities

Password management is a fundamental aspect of identity and access management (IAM), ensuring that users can securely authenticate while minimizing security risks associated with weak or compromised credentials. Despite advancements in authentication technologies, passwords remain a primary method of securing access to enterprise systems, cloud applications, and sensitive data. However, poor password practices, such as reusing credentials, using weak passwords, and failing to update them regularly, make organizations vulnerable to credential theft, phishing attacks, and brute-force attempts. Effective password management strategies, combined with self-service capabilities, enhance security while improving user experience and reducing IT administrative burden.

A well-structured password management policy enforces strong password creation rules, requiring users to create complex, unique passwords that resist common attacks. Organizations implement policies that mandate a combination of uppercase and lowercase letters, numbers, and special characters, ensuring that passwords meet security best practices. Additionally, password length requirements help prevent dictionary attacks, as longer passwords are significantly harder to crack. Some enterprises also implement passphrases, which encourage users to create memorable but highly secure passwords using multiple words rather than a single complex string.

To address the risks of password reuse and weak credentials, organizations implement password expiration policies and periodic password changes. However, frequent mandatory password resets can lead to user frustration and poor security habits, such as writing down passwords or using predictable variations of previous passwords. Modern security best practices advocate for risk-based password expiration, where passwords are changed only when a security event, such as a breach or suspicious login activity, is detected. Organizations leverage password intelligence tools that scan for compromised credentials exposed in data breaches, prompting users to reset passwords only when necessary.

Self-service password management capabilities empower users to reset or update their passwords without requiring IT intervention. Traditionally, forgotten passwords led to helpdesk tickets, causing delays in access and increasing operational costs. Self-service password reset (SSPR) solutions integrate with IAM platforms, allowing users to securely reset their passwords through multi-factor authentication (MFA), identity verification, or predefined security questions. By enabling self-service password recovery, organizations reduce helpdesk workload while enhancing user convenience.

MFA strengthens password security by requiring users to provide additional authentication factors beyond their passwords. Even if a password is compromised, MFA ensures that unauthorized users cannot access the account without verifying their identity through a second factor, such as a one-time passcode (OTP), biometric authentication, or hardware security key. Many organizations enforce adaptive MFA policies that assess login risk levels, requiring step-up authentication only when unusual activity is detected, such as logins from unrecognized devices or foreign locations.

Password vaults and enterprise password managers help organizations enforce secure password storage and usage. Instead of relying on users to remember multiple credentials, password managers generate, store, and autofill strong passwords across applications. Enterprise password managers integrate with IAM solutions to enforce organizational password policies, ensuring that employees use secure, unique passwords for different accounts. Additionally, password vaulting solutions store privileged credentials in encrypted repositories, restricting access to authorized users and implementing just-in-time (JIT) password retrieval for sensitive accounts.

Single sign-on (SSO) solutions reduce password fatigue by allowing users to access multiple applications with a single set of credentials. SSO eliminates the need to remember multiple passwords, reducing the likelihood of password reuse and improving security posture. Organizations implement SSO with identity federation protocols, such as SAML and OpenID Connect, to authenticate users across cloud applications, SaaS platforms, and on-premises systems seamlessly. By integrating SSO with MFA, organizations further enhance security while simplifying authentication processes for employees, contractors, and partners.

Account lockout and password policy enforcement mechanisms protect against brute-force attacks and unauthorized access attempts. Organizations implement account lockout thresholds that temporarily disable accounts after multiple failed login attempts, preventing automated credential stuffing attacks. However, excessive account lockouts can lead to user frustration and increased IT support requests. Modern IAM solutions incorporate intelligent lockout mechanisms that distinguish between legitimate user mistakes and malicious login attempts, dynamically adjusting lockout policies based on risk assessments.

Self-service password synchronization simplifies password management in hybrid IT environments where users must manage credentials across multiple systems. When a user updates their password in one system, password synchronization ensures that the change propagates across all connected applications, reducing the need to remember multiple passwords. This capability is especially beneficial in organizations with legacy systems that require different authentication credentials. IAM solutions integrate password synchronization with directory services such as Microsoft Active Directory (AD) and cloud identity providers to maintain consistency across authentication environments.

Passwordless authentication is gaining traction as an alternative to traditional password management, leveraging secure authentication methods such as biometrics, cryptographic keys, and FIDO2-based authentication. Organizations adopting passwordless authentication reduce dependency on passwords while improving security and user experience. Employees can authenticate using fingerprint scans, facial recognition, or hardware tokens, eliminating the risks associated with password reuse and phishing attacks. Passwordless authentication is particularly effective when combined with zero-trust security principles, where continuous identity verification ensures secure access to enterprise resources.

Compliance and regulatory requirements emphasize strong password management practices to protect sensitive data and prevent unauthorized access. Regulations such as GDPR, HIPAA, and PCI-DSS mandate the enforcement of password policies, periodic access reviews, and authentication monitoring. Organizations implement audit logging and reporting capabilities to track password-related events, such as failed authentication attempts, password resets, and account lockouts. Automated compliance reporting helps organizations demonstrate adherence to regulatory standards while identifying potential security gaps in password management policies.

AI-driven security analytics enhance password management by detecting anomalous behavior, identifying weak credentials, and predicting security risks. AI-powered IAM platforms analyze login patterns, password reset frequency, and authentication failures to detect potential account compromises. If an AI-driven system identifies suspicious activity, such as a user logging in from multiple locations simultaneously or repeatedly resetting their password, automated response mechanisms trigger additional authentication challenges or temporary access restrictions.

User education and awareness play a crucial role in password security. Organizations implement security training programs to educate employees about phishing threats, secure password creation, and best practices for managing credentials. Regular security awareness campaigns reinforce the importance of avoiding password sharing, recognizing social engineering attacks, and using enterprise-approved password management tools. Encouraging a security-conscious culture reduces the risk of password-related security breaches while fostering proactive identity protection behaviors.

A robust password management strategy, combined with self-service capabilities, improves security, enhances user experience, and reduces administrative overhead. By enforcing strong password policies, integrating self-service password resets, adopting passwordless authentication, and leveraging AI-driven security analytics, organizations strengthen their identity management framework while minimizing risks associated with compromised credentials. As cybersecurity threats continue to evolve, password management solutions remain a critical component of an organization's overall security strategy, ensuring that user identities are protected and access remains secure.

Secure Deprovisioning and Access Revocation

Secure deprovisioning and access revocation are critical components of identity and access management (IAM), ensuring that users no longer retain access to enterprise systems, applications, and data once their employment or engagement with an organization ends. Without an effective deprovisioning process, organizations face security risks such as orphaned accounts, privilege creep, and unauthorized access, which can lead to data breaches, insider threats, and regulatory non-compliance. Automating access revocation and enforcing strict offboarding policies minimize these risks while maintaining operational efficiency and security.

Deprovisioning begins when an employee, contractor, or third-party partner leaves the organization or no longer requires access to certain systems. Traditionally, organizations relied on manual deprovisioning processes, where IT administrators manually disable accounts and revoke permissions. However, this approach is prone to errors and delays, leading to accounts remaining active for extended periods even after user departure. Automated deprovisioning solutions integrate with human resources (HR) systems and identity governance platforms to immediately trigger access revocation upon detecting employment termination or contract completion.

One of the main risks associated with improper deprovisioning is the persistence of orphaned accounts. These are accounts that remain active despite their associated users no longer being employed or contracted by the organization. Orphaned accounts pose a significant security risk, as they can be exploited by attackers to gain unauthorized access to corporate systems. Automated identity lifecycle management solutions mitigate this risk by continuously monitoring inactive accounts, flagging orphaned identities, and automatically disabling or deleting them based on predefined policies.

Just-in-time (JIT) access provisioning enhances security by ensuring that access to critical systems is granted only when needed and revoked immediately when it is no longer required. Instead of providing users with permanent access to privileged accounts, organizations implement JIT policies that allow access on a temporary basis. This approach reduces the attack surface by limiting the exposure of privileged credentials and ensuring that elevated permissions do not persist beyond their intended use.

Role-based access control (RBAC) and attribute-based access control (ABAC) play a crucial role in deprovisioning by ensuring that users are granted access based on their job function and predefined policies.

When an employee transitions to a new role or department, their access rights should be automatically adjusted to reflect their new responsibilities. Failing to revoke previous permissions can result in privilege creep, where users accumulate excessive access rights over time. Automated access reviews and periodic certification processes help identify and remove unnecessary permissions, reducing security vulnerabilities.

Privileged access management (PAM) solutions further strengthen deprovisioning by enforcing strict controls over administrative and high-risk accounts. Privileged users, such as IT administrators and executives, have access to critical systems and sensitive data, making it imperative to revoke their access immediately upon termination. PAM solutions automate privileged access deprovisioning by disabling administrator credentials, revoking session tokens, and resetting passwords for shared accounts. Additionally, PAM tools implement session monitoring and logging to detect any unauthorized access attempts from accounts that should have been deprovisioned.

Cloud environments introduce additional challenges in access revocation, as users often have identities spread across multiple cloud platforms, SaaS applications, and hybrid infrastructures. Unlike traditional on-premises systems where access is managed centrally, cloud-based identities require integration with cloud identity providers such as Microsoft Azure AD, Google Cloud IAM, and AWS IAM. Secure deprovisioning in cloud environments involves automatically revoking OAuth tokens, API keys, and federated access credentials to prevent unauthorized access. Organizations implement cloud access security brokers (CASBs) to monitor and enforce cloud-based access policies, ensuring that deprovisioned users cannot access cloud resources after leaving the organization.

Multi-factor authentication (MFA) policies must also be considered during the deprovisioning process. While MFA adds an extra layer of security for authentication, failing to revoke authentication factors such as mobile app access, security tokens, or biometric enrollment can leave security gaps. Automated IAM solutions ensure that all MFA factors are invalidated when a user's access is revoked, preventing former employees from using saved authentication credentials to regain access.

Regulatory compliance mandates strict access control policies, making secure deprovisioning a legal requirement for many organizations. Regulations such as GDPR, HIPAA, SOX, and NIST 800-53 require businesses to enforce identity governance policies that ensure timely access revocation for terminated employees and third-party users. Compliance audits assess whether organizations properly deprovision accounts and remove unauthorized access, with non-compliance leading to financial penalties and reputational damage. Automated audit trails and access logs provide detailed records of deprovisioning actions, helping organizations demonstrate compliance with regulatory requirements.

Identity analytics and AI-driven security monitoring enhance deprovisioning processes by identifying anomalies and detecting unauthorized access attempts. Machine learning algorithms analyze access patterns to determine whether deprovisioned accounts are still being used or if unauthorized login attempts occur from suspicious locations. If an AI-driven IAM system detects anomalies related to accounts that should have been revoked, automated response mechanisms can immediately disable the account, alert security teams, and initiate forensic investigations.

Deprovisioning must also extend beyond user accounts to include physical access control and third-party integrations. Employees often have access to office buildings, secure facilities, and data centers through access badges, biometric authentication, or keycards. Failing to revoke physical access credentials can lead to security breaches where former employees or contractors gain unauthorized entry to restricted areas. Automated integration between IAM platforms and physical security systems ensures that deprovisioning policies apply to both digital and physical access.

Vendor and contractor access management requires special attention in the deprovisioning process. Unlike full-time employees, third-party users often have temporary access to specific systems, making it essential to enforce time-bound access policies. Organizations implement automated expiration policies that revoke third-party access upon contract completion, reducing the risk of external threats. Periodic reviews of vendor and contractor access help ensure that external users do not retain access beyond their required period.

Secure deprovisioning strategies include implementing real-time access revocation mechanisms that terminate active sessions when a user is offboarded. If a user is logged into critical applications or VPNs at the time of termination, automated IAM solutions can force session termination, preventing continued access even before account deactivation takes effect. Real-time deprovisioning minimizes the risk of data exfiltration by ensuring that users cannot transfer or modify sensitive information after their access is revoked.

Continuous monitoring and policy enforcement ensure that deprovisioning processes remain effective as organizations evolve. Businesses frequently update their IT environments, onboard new applications, and integrate third-party services, requiring identity governance frameworks to adapt accordingly. Regular security assessments, penetration testing, and IAM policy audits help organizations refine their deprovisioning strategies to address emerging threats and compliance requirements.

By integrating secure deprovisioning and access revocation into IAM strategies, organizations strengthen security, prevent insider threats, and maintain compliance with regulatory mandates. Automating these processes reduces human error, enhances operational efficiency, and ensures that user access is revoked promptly and completely when it is no longer required. Effective deprovisioning is a foundational element of identity security, protecting organizations from unauthorized access while maintaining strong identity governance.

Identity Lifecycle Metrics and KPIs

Measuring the effectiveness of identity lifecycle management requires organizations to define and track key performance indicators (KPIs) and metrics that provide insights into identity governance, security, and operational efficiency. Identity lifecycle management involves the processes of provisioning, modifying, and deprovisioning user accounts, ensuring that access is properly controlled throughout a user's tenure with an organization. By leveraging identity lifecycle metrics, businesses can evaluate their IAM strategies, identify inefficiencies, and optimize security policies to minimize risks and enhance compliance.

One of the most important identity lifecycle KPIs is provisioning time, which measures the speed at which new users are granted access to essential systems and applications. Long provisioning times lead to productivity delays, as employees, contractors, or third-party users may be unable to perform their job functions until access is granted. Organizations aim to reduce provisioning time through automation, integrating IAM platforms with HR systems to enable real-time account creation and role-based access assignments. Comparing provisioning time across different departments and access levels helps identify bottlenecks and optimize workflow efficiency.

Another critical metric is accuracy of access provisioning, which evaluates whether users receive the correct permissions based on their job roles and responsibilities. Errors in access provisioning, such as over-provisioning or under-provisioning, can lead to security risks and operational inefficiencies. Over-provisioning increases the likelihood of privilege creep, where users accumulate excessive permissions over time, potentially leading to unauthorized data access. Under-provisioning, on the other hand, disrupts productivity by preventing users from accessing necessary resources. Regular audits and role-based access control (RBAC) reviews help measure and improve access provisioning accuracy.

Access review and certification rates indicate how effectively an organization manages periodic access audits to ensure that only authorized users retain access to enterprise systems. Compliance frameworks such as GDPR, HIPAA, and SOX mandate regular access reviews to verify that user entitlements align with business policies and security requirements. Measuring the percentage of completed access reviews within the required timeframe helps organizations maintain compliance while identifying accounts that require remediation. Automating access certification workflows enhances review completion rates and reduces administrative workload.

Number of orphaned accounts is a crucial security metric that measures the presence of active accounts associated with former employees, contractors, or external partners. Orphaned accounts pose a significant security risk, as attackers can exploit them to gain unauthorized access to sensitive systems. Organizations track the number of orphaned accounts over time, aiming to reduce or eliminate them through automated deprovisioning workflows. Integrating IAM solutions with HR systems ensures that account termination aligns with employment status changes, preventing orphaned accounts from lingering in enterprise directories.

Deprovisioning time is another key metric that measures how quickly user accounts and access rights are revoked after an individual leaves an organization or no longer requires access. Delays in deprovisioning increase the risk of insider threats, as former employees or contractors may retain access to confidential data. Best practices for secure deprovisioning include implementing immediate access revocation upon termination and conducting periodic audits to verify that all former users have been properly offboarded. Organizations that measure and optimize deprovisioning time strengthen their security posture while reducing compliance risks.

Multi-factor authentication (MFA) adoption rate tracks the percentage of users who have enabled or been required to use MFA for authentication. MFA significantly enhances security by adding an extra layer of protection beyond passwords, preventing unauthorized access even if credentials are compromised. Organizations measure MFA adoption to assess whether security policies are effectively enforced across all user groups, including employees, contractors, and privileged users. Increasing MFA adoption through mandatory policies, adaptive authentication, and security awareness campaigns reduces the likelihood of credential-based attacks.

Privileged access management (PAM) effectiveness evaluates how well an organization controls and monitors privileged accounts. This metric includes tracking the percentage of privileged accounts with just-in-time (JIT) access policies, session monitoring enforcement rates, and the frequency of privileged access audits. Since privileged accounts have elevated permissions that could be exploited by attackers, organizations focus on minimizing the number of permanent privileged accounts, enforcing session recording, and rotating administrator credentials regularly. PAM effectiveness KPIs help organizations maintain tight security controls over critical IT assets.

Access request approval time measures the speed at which access requests are reviewed and approved by managers, system owners, or security teams. Lengthy approval times create friction for employees and slow down business operations. Organizations optimize approval workflows by automating access requests, implementing predefined approval policies, and enabling self-service access request portals. Comparing access request approval times across different systems and departments helps organizations identify inefficiencies and streamline decision-making processes.

Rate of access violations and policy breaches provides insight into how often users attempt to access unauthorized systems, violate security policies, or trigger access control alerts. High violation rates may indicate gaps in access policies, ineffective training, or the need for stricter enforcement measures. Organizations use security monitoring tools, anomaly detection systems, and IAM analytics to detect and analyze policy breaches, enabling them to refine access controls and prevent future incidents.

User satisfaction with IAM processes is a qualitative metric that measures how effectively identity management solutions support business operations. Employee feedback on account setup, access request processes, password resets, and authentication experiences helps organizations assess the usability of their IAM platforms. High user frustration levels may indicate excessive security friction, while low engagement with IAM self-service tools may suggest a need for better user education or system improvements. Conducting regular user experience surveys ensures that IAM strategies balance security with productivity.

Identity-related incident response time measures how quickly organizations detect, investigate, and remediate identity security incidents such as account takeovers, unauthorized access attempts, or phishing attacks. Faster response times reduce the impact of security breaches and improve overall cyber resilience. Organizations integrate IAM solutions with security information and event management (SIEM) platforms to enable real-time incident detection and automated response workflows, minimizing the time required to mitigate identity-related threats.

Cost savings from IAM automation assesses the financial impact of automating identity lifecycle processes. Manual identity management tasks, such as user provisioning, access certification, and password resets, consume valuable IT resources and increase operational costs. Organizations calculate cost savings by comparing the reduction in administrative workload, helpdesk tickets, and security incidents before and after IAM automation implementation. Demonstrating cost efficiency strengthens the business case for further IAM investments and optimization initiatives.

Tracking identity lifecycle metrics and KPIs enables organizations to continuously improve their IAM programs, ensuring that user identities are securely managed throughout their lifecycle. By measuring provisioning efficiency, access governance effectiveness, security policy compliance, and user experience, businesses can optimize their identity management strategies to enhance security, streamline operations, and meet regulatory requirements.

Challenges in Identity Lifecycle Management

Identity lifecycle management (ILM) is a complex process that involves creating, maintaining, and deprovisioning user identities across an organization's IT ecosystem. As enterprises expand their digital footprint, managing identities across cloud applications, hybrid environments, and third-party integrations introduces numerous challenges. Organizations must ensure that identities are securely managed while maintaining compliance with regulatory requirements and minimizing security risks. Despite the advancements in identity and access management (IAM) solutions, identity lifecycle management remains a challenging task due to issues such as inconsistent access control, privilege creep, orphaned accounts, integration difficulties, and lack of automation.

One of the most significant challenges in identity lifecycle management is inconsistent identity provisioning across different systems. Organizations use multiple applications, platforms, and directory services to manage identities, making it difficult to maintain a unified approach to user provisioning. When new employees, contractors, or vendors are onboarded, they require immediate access to necessary systems based on their roles and responsibilities.

However, delays in provisioning can hinder productivity, while inconsistencies in assigning permissions can lead to excessive or insufficient access. Manual provisioning processes increase the likelihood of human error, causing security vulnerabilities and inefficiencies.

Another critical issue is privilege creep, which occurs when users accumulate access rights over time due to role changes, project assignments, or system migrations. Without proper governance, employees may retain permissions that are no longer required, creating security risks. Privilege creep increases the attack surface, allowing cybercriminals or malicious insiders to exploit excessive permissions for unauthorized activities. Organizations must implement strict access review policies and role-based access control (RBAC) to ensure that users only retain permissions necessary for their job functions. However, maintaining RBAC policies across dynamic business environments requires continuous monitoring and policy adjustments.

The presence of orphaned accounts is a persistent challenge in identity lifecycle management. Orphaned accounts are user accounts that remain active after an employee, contractor, or vendor has left the organization. These accounts create security risks because they can be exploited by attackers to gain unauthorized access to sensitive systems and data. Orphaned accounts often result from poor deprovisioning processes, where HR and IT systems are not synchronized, leading to delays or oversight in revoking access. Automated deprovisioning workflows integrated with HR platforms and IAM solutions can help mitigate this risk, but many organizations struggle with achieving seamless identity synchronization.

Organizations operating in hybrid IT environments face integration challenges when managing identities across on-premises and cloud-based systems. Legacy IAM solutions were designed for centralized, on-premises environments, making it difficult to extend identity management capabilities to modern cloud applications. The lack of integration between legacy IAM platforms and cloud identity providers, such as Microsoft Azure AD, Google Cloud Identity, and AWS IAM, results in fragmented identity management processes. Organizations must adopt identity federation, single sign-on (SSO), and cloud access security broker (CASB) solutions to bridge the gap between legacy systems and cloud environments.

Another major challenge is lack of automation in identity lifecycle processes, leading to inefficiencies and security vulnerabilities. Many organizations still rely on manual identity management workflows, which are slow, error-prone, and difficult to scale. Without automation, IT teams struggle to keep up with access requests, approval workflows, and access reviews. Automated IAM solutions streamline identity provisioning, enforce policy-based access controls, and execute real-time deprovisioning. However, implementing IAM automation requires significant investment in technology, integration, and governance frameworks, making it a challenging transition for many enterprises.

Ensuring identity governance and compliance remains a significant challenge, particularly for organizations that must adhere to industry regulations such as GDPR, HIPAA, SOX, and PCI-DSS. Regulatory requirements mandate strict access controls, periodic access reviews, and audit trails for user identities. Failure to enforce proper identity governance policies can result in non-compliance, financial penalties, and reputational damage. Many organizations struggle to implement identity governance frameworks that provide visibility into access rights, enforce least privilege policies, and automate compliance reporting. IAM solutions with built-in compliance dashboards and automated reporting capabilities help address these challenges, but organizations must ensure that their identity governance strategies remain aligned with evolving regulatory requirements.

The increasing use of non-human identities in modern IT environments further complicates identity lifecycle management. Service accounts, API keys, robotic process automation (RPA) bots, and cloud workloads require identity authentication and access controls, similar to human users. However, many organizations lack visibility into how these non-human identities are managed, leading to security risks. Hardcoded credentials, excessive permissions, and unmanaged service accounts create potential attack vectors for cybercriminals. Implementing machine identity governance, secrets management, and automated credential rotation helps address these risks, but organizations must integrate these capabilities into their existing IAM frameworks.

Organizations also face challenges in managing identities in remote and hybrid work environments. The shift to remote work has increased reliance on cloud applications, VPNs, and remote authentication mechanisms, making identity security more complex. Traditional perimeter-based security models are no longer effective in protecting distributed workforces. Zero Trust security principles, which enforce continuous identity verification and least privilege access, help mitigate remote access risks. However, implementing Zero Trust requires organizations to adopt risk-based authentication, adaptive access controls, and identity analytics, which can be resource-intensive and difficult to operationalize.

Another issue in identity lifecycle management is poor user experience in authentication and access processes. Complex password policies, frequent authentication requirements, and inefficient access request workflows can frustrate users, leading to poor security practices such as password reuse and unauthorized workarounds. Organizations must strike a balance between security and usability by implementing frictionless authentication mechanisms such as biometric authentication, passwordless login, and SSO. Self-service access request portals and automated approval workflows also improve the user experience while maintaining security controls.

Lack of real-time identity monitoring and threat detection exposes organizations to security breaches caused by compromised credentials, insider threats, and anomalous access behaviors. Traditional identity management systems rely on periodic access reviews, which may not detect suspicious activity in time to prevent an attack. AI-driven identity analytics enhance security by continuously monitoring user behavior, detecting anomalies, and triggering automated security responses. However, organizations must integrate identity analytics with security operations centers (SOCs) and SIEM solutions to achieve real-time threat detection and response.

Despite these challenges, organizations can improve identity lifecycle management by adopting IAM best practices, leveraging automation, and integrating identity governance solutions. Implementing a unified identity strategy that spans on-premises and cloud environments, enforcing role-based access policies, and continuously monitoring identity activities helps organizations strengthen security while maintaining compliance. Overcoming these identity lifecycle management challenges requires a proactive approach, investment in modern IAM technologies, and continuous adaptation to evolving security threats and regulatory requirements.

The Role of Identity in Digital Transformation

Identity plays a central role in digital transformation, enabling organizations to securely and efficiently adapt to new technologies, business models, and customer expectations. As enterprises shift to cloud-based infrastructures, adopt remote work environments, and integrate emerging technologies, identity and access management (IAM) becomes the foundation for securing digital interactions. Digital transformation involves not only technological upgrades but also a fundamental shift in how businesses operate, requiring identity management solutions that support seamless, secure, and user-friendly experiences across multiple platforms.

One of the primary drivers of digital transformation is the transition from on-premises systems to cloud environments. Cloud computing enables businesses to scale operations, improve agility, and reduce IT infrastructure costs. However, managing identities across cloud-based applications, hybrid environments, and on-premises systems presents significant security and operational challenges. Identity federation and single sign-on (SSO) allow organizations to provide users with secure, unified access to multiple applications without requiring multiple credentials. Federated identity management ensures that employees, customers, and partners can authenticate seamlessly across cloud platforms while maintaining security policies.

Zero Trust security is another key aspect of digital transformation that relies on identity as the primary control mechanism. The traditional perimeter-based security model, where users inside a corporate network were inherently trusted, is no longer effective in protecting against modern cyber threats. Zero Trust enforces continuous identity verification, least privilege access, and real-time monitoring to prevent unauthorized access. Organizations implementing Zero Trust architectures leverage multi-factor authentication (MFA), risk-based access controls, and behavioral analytics to verify users, devices, and applications before granting access to critical resources.

The shift to remote and hybrid work has further highlighted the importance of identity in digital transformation. Employees, contractors, and third-party partners now access enterprise applications from various locations, devices, and networks. Organizations must ensure that remote access is secure, frictionless, and scalable to accommodate a distributed workforce. Identity-centric security measures, such as adaptive authentication, device trust assessments, and conditional access policies, allow organizations to enforce security controls without compromising productivity. By centralizing identity management, businesses can provide employees with seamless access to work applications while protecting sensitive data from cyber threats.

Customer identity and access management (CIAM) plays a crucial role in digital transformation by enhancing customer experiences and securing digital interactions. Businesses that operate in e-commerce, banking, healthcare, and digital services require robust identity verification processes to prevent fraud, protect customer data, and comply with regulatory requirements. CIAM solutions enable organizations to implement frictionless authentication experiences, such as social logins, passwordless authentication, and biometric verification, ensuring that customers can access services conveniently while maintaining security. By integrating identity verification with customer analytics, businesses can personalize user experiences, improve engagement, and build customer trust.

Artificial intelligence (AI) and machine learning (ML) are transforming identity management by enabling intelligent security controls and predictive analytics. AI-driven IAM solutions analyze user behavior patterns, detect anomalies, and automate risk-based authentication decisions. Machine learning algorithms help organizations identify suspicious login attempts, detect compromised credentials, and prevent account takeovers before they occur. By integrating AI-powered identity analytics with security information and event management (SIEM) systems, businesses can enhance threat detection and automate responses to identity-based attacks.

The role of identity in digital transformation extends beyond users to include non-human identities, such as API keys, service accounts, and robotic process automation (RPA) bots. Modern IT ecosystems rely on automated workflows, cloud-native applications, and interconnected systems that require secure identity management. Organizations must implement strong authentication, access controls, and credential management solutions for machine identities to prevent unauthorized access and credential misuse. Automated identity lifecycle management ensures that non-human identities follow the same security standards as human users, reducing the risk of identity-related vulnerabilities.

Regulatory compliance is another key consideration in digital transformation, as businesses must ensure that identity management practices align with industry regulations such as GDPR, HIPAA, PCI-DSS, and SOC 2. Compliance frameworks require organizations to implement strict access controls, enforce data protection policies, and maintain audit trails for identity-related activities. Automated identity governance solutions enable businesses to conduct access reviews, enforce least privilege policies, and generate compliance reports in real-time. By integrating identity management with compliance initiatives, organizations can mitigate regulatory risks while maintaining secure digital operations.

Identity plays a vital role in digital ecosystems that involve multiple stakeholders, including employees, customers, suppliers, and business partners. As organizations expand their digital services, they must manage external identities securely while providing seamless access to collaborative platforms. Identity federation, business-to-business (B2B) IAM solutions, and delegated access controls allow enterprises to securely connect with external users without exposing sensitive corporate data. By leveraging identity-centric security models, businesses can foster digital collaboration while maintaining strict access policies.

Blockchain-based identity solutions are emerging as a potential component of digital transformation, offering decentralized identity management capabilities. Decentralized identity frameworks allow users to control their digital identities without relying on centralized authorities, reducing the risks associated with data breaches and identity theft. Organizations exploring blockchain for identity management can leverage self-sovereign identity (SSI) models, verifiable credentials, and distributed ledger technology to enhance security, privacy, and user control over identity data. While decentralized identity is still in its early stages, it presents opportunities for businesses to improve identity verification and authentication processes.

Identity orchestration is another key aspect of digital transformation, enabling organizations to manage identity interactions across multiple platforms, applications, and authentication providers. Businesses adopt identity orchestration platforms to create seamless authentication experiences, integrate various IAM solutions, and enforce security policies dynamically. By orchestrating identity workflows, organizations can reduce authentication friction, streamline access management, and enhance security posture across diverse digital ecosystems.

As digital transformation accelerates, organizations must continuously evolve their identity management strategies to address emerging security challenges, technological advancements, and evolving user expectations. Identity serves as the foundation for secure digital operations, enabling businesses to innovate while protecting sensitive assets. By integrating IAM solutions with cloud platforms, AI-driven analytics, regulatory compliance frameworks, and decentralized identity models, organizations can build resilient, scalable, and secure digital ecosystems.

Emphasizing identity as a core component of digital transformation ensures that businesses can adapt to changing security landscapes, enhance user experiences, and maintain regulatory compliance while leveraging new technologies. Identity-driven security architectures enable organizations to manage digital interactions securely, reduce cyber risks, and support seamless access to digital services in an increasingly connected world.

Managing Identity for Mergers and Acquisitions

Managing identity during mergers and acquisitions (M&A) is a complex process that requires careful planning, integration, and security considerations. When two organizations merge or one company acquires another, their identity and access management (IAM) systems must be consolidated to ensure seamless access for employees, maintain security, and support business continuity. Identity management plays a crucial role in enabling a smooth transition, preventing security risks, and ensuring compliance with regulatory requirements. Without a well-structured identity integration strategy, organizations may face operational disruptions, security vulnerabilities, and increased costs associated with managing disparate IAM environments.

One of the first challenges in identity management during M&A is assessing existing IAM infrastructures. The merging entities often have different IAM solutions, authentication methods, directory services, and access control models. Some organizations may use traditional on-premises Active Directory (AD), while others rely on cloud-based identity providers such as Azure AD, Okta, or Google Workspace. Understanding the differences in identity architectures, user repositories, and authentication mechanisms is critical to developing a unified IAM strategy that supports both organizations.

User identity reconciliation is a fundamental step in integrating IAM systems. Employees from both organizations may have different usernames, email addresses, and access credentials that need to be standardized. Duplicate accounts must be identified and resolved to avoid conflicts, ensuring that users maintain access to the necessary applications without disruption. Automated identity reconciliation tools help match user identities across systems by analyzing attributes such as employee ID, email, and organizational role. By consolidating duplicate identities and standardizing naming conventions, organizations create a unified identity structure that facilitates seamless authentication and access management.

A key priority in M&A identity management is ensuring secure access provisioning for employees during the transition period. Without proper access controls, employees may either lose access to critical business systems or gain excessive permissions due to misconfigured access policies. Implementing a role-based access control (RBAC) model helps organizations define and assign permissions based on job functions, reducing the risk of privilege creep. If one company has a more mature IAM framework, its access control policies can serve as the foundation for the newly merged organization. Organizations should also enforce least privilege access, ensuring that users receive only the permissions necessary for their roles.

The authentication process must also be unified to avoid security gaps and improve user experience. Organizations involved in M&A may have different authentication mechanisms, including single sign-on (SSO), multi-factor authentication (MFA), and federated identity solutions. Aligning authentication standards ensures that users can securely access applications across the merged infrastructure. If one company relies on MFA for authentication while the other does not, it is essential to enforce MFA across the entire organization to enhance security. Identity federation enables seamless authentication between legacy and cloud environments, reducing the need for employees to manage multiple login credentials.

Privileged access management (PAM) is particularly important during M&A, as IT administrators, security teams, and third-party consultants require elevated access to integrate systems, transfer data, and configure IAM settings. Without proper oversight, privileged accounts can become a target for attackers seeking to exploit security gaps. Implementing just-in-time (JIT) access controls, session monitoring, and privileged session recording helps organizations track administrative activities and prevent unauthorized access. Security teams should also conduct audits to identify and revoke unnecessary privileged accounts inherited from the acquired entity.

Compliance with regulatory and security frameworks is another critical consideration in M&A identity management. Organizations must ensure that IAM policies align with industry regulations such as GDPR, HIPAA, SOX, and PCI-DSS. The merging companies may have different compliance requirements based on their industries and geographic locations, requiring a harmonized approach to identity governance. IAM solutions should enforce policy-driven access controls, maintain audit logs of identity-related activities, and generate compliance reports to demonstrate adherence to regulatory standards. Failure to address compliance risks during identity integration can result in legal penalties and reputational damage.

Identity lifecycle management plays a key role in maintaining security and efficiency throughout the M&A process. Employees may change roles, transfer to different departments, or leave the organization entirely, requiring adjustments to their access rights. Automating identity lifecycle workflows ensures that users are provisioned, modified, and deprovisioned in a timely manner. Deprovisioning former employees from the acquired organization must be handled carefully to prevent orphaned accounts that could be exploited by malicious actors. Organizations should integrate IAM systems with HR platforms to synchronize employment status changes and enforce real-time access revocation.

Organizations must also address non-human identities, such as service accounts, API keys, and machine identities. M&A activities often involve the integration of automated workflows, cloud applications, and software systems that rely on non-human identities for authentication and data exchange. Conducting an inventory of service accounts and implementing secrets management solutions helps secure machine identities, preventing unauthorized access to critical infrastructure. API security policies should also be reviewed to ensure that third-party integrations comply with the organization's security standards.

User experience and change management are essential factors in identity integration. Employees from the acquired company may experience disruptions in their daily workflows if IAM changes are not communicated effectively. Organizations should provide clear guidance on authentication changes, password resets, and access request processes to minimize confusion. Self-service IAM portals enable employees to manage their own credentials, request access to applications, and resolve authentication issues without requiring IT intervention. Conducting training sessions and providing documentation on IAM best practices helps users adapt to the new identity framework.

Post-merger identity audits help organizations assess the effectiveness of IAM integration and identify potential security gaps. Conducting access certification reviews ensures that users retain only the necessary permissions for their job functions. Security teams should analyze IAM logs, monitor for suspicious activity, and implement behavioral analytics to detect anomalous authentication patterns. Continuous identity monitoring allows organizations to proactively identify and mitigate security threats that may arise from the M&A transition.

Integrating identity management during mergers and acquisitions requires a strategic approach that balances security, compliance, and operational efficiency. By conducting identity assessments, standardizing authentication methods, enforcing access controls, and automating identity lifecycle management, organizations can create a unified IAM framework that supports seamless business operations. Identity remains a critical component of M&A success, ensuring that employees maintain secure access to business systems while minimizing security risks and compliance challenges.

Customer Identity and Access Management (CIAM)

Customer Identity and Access Management (CIAM) is a specialized branch of identity management focused on securing and managing customer identities while ensuring seamless and personalized user experiences. Unlike traditional IAM systems designed for internal employees, CIAM solutions cater to external users, such as customers, partners, and vendors, who require access to digital services, applications, and platforms. As businesses expand their digital presence, CIAM plays a critical role in balancing security, privacy, and user convenience, enabling organizations to provide secure authentication, authorization, and identity governance across multiple channels.

One of the core components of CIAM is secure customer authentication, which ensures that users can access their accounts while preventing unauthorized access. Traditional authentication methods, such as username and password combinations, are no longer sufficient due to the increasing sophistication of credential theft, phishing attacks, and account takeovers. Organizations implement multi-factor authentication (MFA), biometric authentication, and passwordless login to enhance security while maintaining a frictionless user experience. Adaptive authentication further strengthens security by analyzing risk signals such as device reputation, login behavior, and geographic location to determine whether additional authentication steps are necessary.

Single sign-on (SSO) is another critical feature of CIAM, enabling customers to use a single set of credentials to access multiple applications and services without needing to log in repeatedly. SSO reduces login friction, improves user convenience, and minimizes password fatigue. Businesses that operate multiple digital services, such as e-commerce platforms, financial portals, and mobile applications, benefit from SSO by providing a seamless authentication experience across their ecosystem. Identity federation protocols like SAML, OpenID Connect (OIDC), and OAuth 2.0 facilitate secure authentication and authorization across different platforms.

CIAM also focuses on user registration and onboarding, ensuring that new customers can create accounts easily while verifying their identities securely. Self-service registration portals allow users to sign up using various methods, such as email verification, phone number confirmation, or social logins from providers like Google, Apple, and Facebook. Progressive profiling enhances the onboarding experience by collecting customer information gradually, reducing the need for users to fill out lengthy forms during initial registration. This approach improves conversion rates while allowing businesses to gather valuable customer insights over time.

Identity proofing and fraud prevention are crucial aspects of CIAM, particularly in industries such as banking, healthcare, and e-commerce, where verifying customer identities is essential to prevent fraudulent activities. Organizations implement identity verification technologies, including document scanning, facial recognition, and AI-driven fraud detection, to ensure that users are who they claim to be. By integrating fraud detection systems with CIAM platforms, businesses can analyze behavioral patterns, detect suspicious activities, and enforce risk-based authentication policies to prevent identity fraud and account takeovers.

Privacy and compliance with data protection regulations are fundamental considerations in CIAM. Organizations handling customer identities must comply with global data privacy laws, such as GDPR, CCPA, and PSD2, which mandate strict controls over personal data collection, storage, and processing. CIAM solutions enforce customer consent management, allowing users to control how their data is used, manage their preferences, and opt-in or opt-out of data-sharing agreements. Transparent privacy policies, encryption of personal data, and secure storage practices ensure compliance with regulatory requirements while building customer trust.

Personalization and customer engagement are additional benefits of CIAM, enabling organizations to deliver customized experiences based on user preferences, behaviors, and interactions. By integrating CIAM with customer relationship management (CRM) and marketing automation platforms, businesses can leverage identity data to provide personalized content, product recommendations, and targeted promotions. Identity-driven personalization enhances customer satisfaction, increases engagement, and strengthens brand loyalty.

Self-service account management empowers customers to manage their own identities, reducing reliance on customer support teams for account-related tasks. CIAM platforms offer self-service portals where users can update their profiles, reset passwords, enable MFA, review account activity, and manage privacy settings. Providing customers with control over their identity information enhances trust and improves the overall user experience.

Cross-platform and omnichannel identity management is essential in CIAM, ensuring that users can authenticate and access services consistently across web applications, mobile devices, smart TVs, and IoT-enabled systems. Organizations implement device-based authentication and persistent sessions to enable seamless access across multiple touchpoints. Whether customers log in from a mobile app or a web browser, their identity experience remains consistent, enhancing usability and engagement.

API security and identity federation play a significant role in CIAM, particularly as businesses integrate third-party applications, payment gateways, and partner ecosystems. Organizations use API-based authentication and authorization mechanisms, such as OAuth 2.0, to secure customer data and ensure that external applications only access authorized resources. Identity federation enables businesses to extend authentication to partners and third-party services while maintaining centralized identity governance.

Threat intelligence and anomaly detection enhance security in CIAM by continuously monitoring user activity for signs of fraudulent behavior, unauthorized access attempts, or compromised credentials. AI-driven security analytics analyze login patterns, device fingerprints, and transaction history to identify potential threats in real time. When suspicious activity is detected, CIAM platforms enforce adaptive security measures, such as step-up authentication, account locking, or risk-based access restrictions, to prevent security breaches.

Scalability and performance are critical considerations in CIAM, especially for enterprises managing millions of customer identities. CIAM solutions must handle high volumes of authentication requests, registration events, and API calls without compromising performance. Cloud-based CIAM platforms provide scalability, redundancy, and high availability to support peak traffic loads, ensuring a seamless user experience even during high-demand periods, such as sales events or product launches.

Customer identity lifecycle management ensures that identities are created, updated, and removed securely throughout their lifecycle. CIAM solutions automate user lifecycle processes, including account provisioning, profile updates, and access revocation. When customers close their accounts or request data deletion, CIAM platforms ensure that personal data is securely erased in compliance with data privacy regulations. Automated lifecycle management helps businesses maintain data integrity while reducing security risks associated with inactive accounts.

Organizations implementing CIAM must focus on security, usability, and compliance to build a trusted digital identity ecosystem. By integrating secure authentication mechanisms, enforcing privacy controls, and leveraging identity-driven personalization, businesses enhance customer trust while protecting against identity-related threats. CIAM serves as the foundation for secure digital interactions, enabling organizations to provide seamless, scalable, and personalized experiences for their customers across digital platforms.

Identity as a Service (IDaaS)

Identity as a Service (IDaaS) is a cloud-based identity and access management (IAM) solution that provides authentication, authorization, and identity governance capabilities as a service. Organizations increasingly rely on IDaaS to secure digital identities, manage access to enterprise applications, and enforce security policies across cloud and on-premises environments. As businesses embrace cloud computing, remote work, and hybrid IT infrastructures, IDaaS solutions offer scalability, automation, and enhanced security while reducing the complexity of managing identity lifecycles.

One of the primary benefits of IDaaS is cloud-based authentication, which eliminates the need for on-premises identity management infrastructure. Traditional IAM solutions require organizations to maintain servers, configure authentication protocols, and manage user directories manually. With IDaaS, authentication processes are handled through cloud-based identity providers, allowing users to access applications securely from any location. Organizations leverage IDaaS to enable single sign-on (SSO), multi-factor authentication (MFA), and federated identity management, ensuring seamless and secure access across multiple platforms.

Single sign-on (SSO) is a core feature of IDaaS, allowing users to authenticate once and access multiple applications without re-entering credentials. By integrating with SAML, OpenID Connect (OIDC), and OAuth 2.0, IDaaS platforms provide centralized authentication for cloud-based and on-premises applications. SSO enhances security by reducing the number of passwords users need to remember while improving productivity by streamlining authentication workflows. Organizations use IDaaS-powered SSO to simplify access to software-as-a-service (SaaS) applications, enterprise portals, and third-party services.

Multi-factor authentication (MFA) is another critical security feature of IDaaS, protecting user identities from credential-based attacks. Instead of relying solely on passwords, IDaaS platforms enforce additional authentication factors, such as one-time passcodes (OTP), biometric verification, security tokens, and push notifications. Adaptive MFA enhances security by dynamically adjusting authentication requirements based on contextual risk factors, such as device trust, login location, and behavioral analytics. Organizations implement IDaaS-driven MFA to safeguard sensitive data, prevent phishing attacks, and comply with regulatory requirements.

IDaaS solutions also support identity federation, enabling users to authenticate across multiple organizations, cloud platforms, and external service providers. Identity federation allows businesses to establish trust relationships between identity providers (IdPs) and service providers (SPs), ensuring seamless authentication across disparate systems. By leveraging federated identity standards, such as SAML and OpenID Connect, organizations eliminate the need for redundant user credentials and improve access management efficiency. Federated authentication is particularly valuable for enterprises with multi-cloud deployments, business partnerships, and supply chain integrations.

Identity lifecycle management is a core function of IDaaS, automating user provisioning, role-based access control (RBAC), and access revocation. Organizations integrate IDaaS platforms with human resources (HR) systems to streamline onboarding and offboarding processes. When a new employee is hired, IDaaS automatically creates user accounts, assigns appropriate permissions, and provisions access based on predefined policies. When an employee leaves the organization, IDaaS ensures that all associated accounts are deactivated promptly, reducing the risk of orphaned accounts and privilege creep.

Access governance and compliance are essential components of IDaaS, enabling organizations to enforce security policies, conduct access reviews, and generate audit reports. Regulatory frameworks, such as GDPR, HIPAA, SOX, and PCI-DSS, require organizations to maintain strict identity governance practices, ensuring that only authorized users can access sensitive data. IDaaS platforms provide built-in compliance dashboards, automated policy enforcement, and audit logging, allowing security teams to track identity-related activities and detect policy violations in real time.

IDaaS enhances privileged access management (PAM) by securing administrator credentials, enforcing least privilege policies, and monitoring high-risk user activities. Organizations implement just-in-time (JIT) privileged access through IDaaS, granting temporary administrative permissions only when necessary. Session recording, keystroke logging, and behavioral analytics further strengthen security by detecting unauthorized privilege escalations. By integrating PAM with IDaaS, organizations mitigate insider threats and prevent cybercriminals from exploiting privileged accounts.

Cloud security integration is another key advantage of IDaaS, enabling organizations to extend identity-based security controls across hybrid and multi-cloud environments. IDaaS platforms integrate with cloud access security brokers (CASBs), endpoint detection and response (EDR) solutions, and zero trust security architectures to enforce risk-based access policies. By continuously monitoring authentication patterns, device compliance, and user behavior, IDaaS strengthens security across distributed IT ecosystems.

Passwordless authentication is an emerging capability within IDaaS, eliminating reliance on traditional passwords by leveraging biometric authentication, cryptographic keys, and FIDO2-based authentication. Passwordless authentication improves security by preventing credential theft while enhancing the user experience by reducing login friction. Organizations adopting passwordless authentication through IDaaS eliminate password fatigue, reduce helpdesk costs, and mitigate risks associated with weak or reused passwords.

The scalability of IDaaS makes it an ideal solution for enterprises managing large user populations, including employees, customers, partners, and IoT devices. Unlike traditional IAM systems that require significant infrastructure investments, IDaaS operates on a pay-as-you-go model, allowing organizations to scale identity services dynamically based on business needs. Cloud-based IAM solutions also provide high availability, redundancy, and failover capabilities, ensuring uninterrupted authentication services even during peak demand periods.

IDaaS platforms incorporate AI-driven security analytics to detect identity-based threats, anomalous login behavior, and fraudulent authentication attempts. By analyzing authentication patterns, access requests, and privilege escalations, machine learning algorithms identify security risks in real time, enabling automated responses to prevent identity fraud and account takeovers. AI-powered IDaaS solutions enhance threat intelligence by correlating identity events with broader security data, improving an organization's ability to defend against sophisticated cyberattacks.

Organizations transitioning to IDaaS must consider integration challenges, data residency requirements, and vendor lock-in risks. Seamless integration with existing IAM frameworks, enterprise applications, and security tools is critical for ensuring smooth identity migration. Compliance with data protection regulations requires organizations to evaluate where identity data is stored and processed, ensuring that IDaaS providers adhere to jurisdictional privacy laws. Vendor lock-in concerns can be addressed by selecting IDaaS solutions that support open standards and interoperability, allowing businesses to switch providers without major disruptions.

As identity security becomes a top priority for digital enterprises, IDaaS continues to evolve, providing scalable, intelligent, and secure identity management solutions. By adopting IDaaS, organizations improve authentication efficiency, enhance security posture, and simplify identity governance across cloud, hybrid, and on-premises environments. Identity as a Service is no longer just an alternative to traditional IAM—it is becoming the standard for modern identity management in an increasingly connected digital world.

Implementing Identity Lifecycle in Large Enterprises

Implementing identity lifecycle management in large enterprises presents significant challenges due to the complexity of managing thousands or even millions of user identities across multiple systems, applications, and locations. A well-structured identity lifecycle management (ILM) framework ensures that users have appropriate access throughout their tenure while maintaining security, compliance, and operational efficiency. Large enterprises must integrate identity lifecycle processes with human resources (HR) systems, automate provisioning and deprovisioning, enforce strict access controls, and continuously monitor identity-related activities to minimize security risks.

One of the first steps in implementing identity lifecycle management in large enterprises is establishing a centralized identity repository. Large organizations typically operate across hybrid IT environments that include on-premises directories, cloud identity providers, and third-party applications. Without a centralized identity repository, managing identities becomes fragmented, leading to inconsistencies in user access and security controls. Enterprises integrate identity lifecycle management with directory services such as Microsoft Active Directory (AD), Azure AD, and cloud-based identity platforms to create a unified identity framework that provides visibility and control over all user accounts.

Automating user provisioning is essential for reducing administrative overhead and ensuring timely access for new employees, contractors, and business partners. Large enterprises cannot rely on manual provisioning, as delays in granting access can impact productivity and increase security risks. Identity lifecycle automation integrates IAM solutions with HR systems such as Workday, SAP SuccessFactors, and Oracle HCM to trigger provisioning workflows based on employment status changes. When a new user is added to the HR system, ILM processes automatically create accounts, assign roles, and provision access to enterprise applications based on predefined policies.

Role-based access control (RBAC) and attribute-based access control (ABAC) play a crucial role in large-scale identity lifecycle management. With thousands of employees performing diverse job functions, enterprises must ensure that access is granted based on predefined roles, attributes, and security policies. RBAC assigns permissions based on job roles, ensuring that employees receive access only to the systems they need. ABAC enhances this model by considering additional attributes such as department, geographic location, security clearance, and project assignments. Implementing RBAC and ABAC across an enterprise-wide identity framework reduces privilege creep and enforces least privilege access principles.

Identity synchronization across multiple systems is another challenge for large enterprises. Employees require access to numerous applications, including cloud-based SaaS platforms, internal databases, collaboration tools, and industry-specific software. Without proper synchronization, identity attributes such as name changes, department transfers, or job title updates may not propagate across all systems, leading to inconsistencies. Enterprises implement identity federation and automated identity synchronization to ensure that changes made in one system reflect across all integrated platforms.

Self-service IAM portals enhance efficiency by allowing employees to manage their own identity-related requests, reducing dependency on IT administrators. Large organizations benefit from self-service password resets, access request workflows, and identity verification tools that empower users while maintaining security. Automated approval workflows route access requests to managers or security teams for review, ensuring that requests are granted based on business policies. Self-service capabilities improve user experience while decreasing administrative workload and helpdesk costs.

Multi-factor authentication (MFA) and adaptive authentication are critical for securing identity lifecycle processes in large enterprises. Given the scale of user identities, enterprises are prime targets for credential-based attacks such as phishing, brute force attacks, and account takeovers. MFA enforces additional security layers by requiring users to verify their identities using methods such as one-time passcodes (OTP), biometric authentication, or security tokens. Adaptive authentication enhances security by analyzing risk factors such as device reputation, login behavior, geographic location, and network security posture, adjusting authentication requirements dynamically.

Privileged access management (PAM) is a crucial component of identity lifecycle management in large enterprises, ensuring that administrative and high-risk accounts are securely managed. Privileged users, such as system administrators, IT security teams, and executive leadership, require enhanced security controls to prevent unauthorized access and insider threats. Enterprises implement just-in-time (JIT) privileged access, session monitoring, and keystroke logging to enforce strict access policies for privileged accounts. By integrating PAM with identity lifecycle management, enterprises reduce the risk of compromised administrator credentials.

Deprovisioning and access revocation must be handled with precision to prevent security risks associated with orphaned accounts and privilege retention. Large enterprises often experience high employee turnover, contract expirations, and third-party collaborations, making it critical to revoke access immediately upon user departure. Automating deprovisioning workflows ensures that inactive accounts are disabled in real-time, preventing unauthorized access. Enterprises also conduct periodic access reviews and certification campaigns to identify and remove unnecessary permissions, ensuring that only active employees retain access.

Regulatory compliance and identity governance are essential aspects of identity lifecycle management in large enterprises. Businesses must comply with GDPR, HIPAA, SOX, PCI-DSS, ISO 27001, and NIST security frameworks, requiring strict controls over identity access and data protection. Automated compliance reporting, access audits, and policy enforcement mechanisms ensure that enterprises meet regulatory standards while maintaining transparency in identity-related activities. By implementing real-time identity monitoring, automated policy enforcement, and forensic analysis, organizations reduce compliance risks and enhance security posture.

Identity analytics and AI-driven security monitoring enhance identity lifecycle management by detecting anomalies, identifying risks, and predicting security threats. AI-powered IAM solutions analyze authentication patterns, access behavior, and privilege escalations to detect unusual activities, such as unauthorized login attempts, account sharing, or suspicious privilege changes. Machine learning algorithms improve identity threat detection by correlating identity events with security intelligence, allowing enterprises to respond to identity-based threats in real time.

Cloud-based identity lifecycle management solutions enable large enterprises to extend IAM capabilities across hybrid and multi-cloud environments. Many enterprises operate in distributed infrastructures, requiring cloud-native IAM platforms such as Identity as a Service (IDaaS) to manage identities at scale. Cloud IAM solutions integrate with cloud access security brokers (CASBs), zero trust security architectures, and cloud-native security controls to enforce consistent identity governance across on-premises, cloud, and SaaS applications.

Business continuity and disaster recovery considerations are essential for large enterprises implementing identity lifecycle management. IAM systems must ensure high availability, fault tolerance, and failover mechanisms to prevent disruptions in authentication and access management. Organizations deploy redundant identity infrastructure, implement disaster recovery plans, and conduct regular IAM resilience testing to ensure that identity lifecycle processes remain functional during system failures or cyber incidents.

Successfully implementing identity lifecycle management in large enterprises requires a combination of automation, security controls, regulatory compliance, and user-centric solutions. By integrating IAM with HR systems, automating provisioning and deprovisioning, enforcing adaptive authentication, and leveraging AI-driven identity analytics, enterprises can effectively manage user identities, enhance security, and optimize operational efficiency at scale. Identity lifecycle management is not only a security requirement but a strategic necessity for organizations looking to maintain a resilient, compliant, and future-proof identity framework.

Best Practices for Identity Lifecycle Policy Design

Designing an effective identity lifecycle policy is essential for organizations to manage user identities securely, ensure compliance, and streamline access control processes. Identity lifecycle management (ILM) encompasses the creation, modification, and removal of user accounts across an enterprise's IT ecosystem. A well-structured policy ensures that identities are properly governed, access is granted based on business needs, and security risks associated with orphaned accounts, privilege creep, and unauthorized access are minimized. Organizations must implement identity lifecycle policies that align with security best practices, regulatory requirements, and operational efficiency goals.

One of the foundational best practices in identity lifecycle policy design is defining clear identity governance roles and responsibilities. Organizations must establish clear ownership over identity management processes, ensuring that HR teams, IT administrators, security teams, and compliance officers understand their respective roles. HR teams initiate identity creation based on employment status changes, IT teams enforce provisioning and deprovisioning workflows, and security teams monitor access controls. By assigning accountability at each stage of the identity lifecycle, organizations can ensure consistent enforcement of policies and prevent identity-related security gaps.

Automating identity provisioning and deprovisioning is a critical component of an effective lifecycle policy. Manual account management processes are inefficient, error-prone, and increase security risks due to delays in access provisioning or revocation. Organizations should integrate ILM policies with human resources (HR) systems to automate user onboarding, ensuring that new employees, contractors, and vendors receive appropriate access immediately upon hire. Automated deprovisioning ensures that user accounts are disabled promptly when individuals leave the organization, reducing the risk of orphaned accounts being exploited for unauthorized access.

Implementing role-based access control (RBAC) and attribute-based access control (ABAC) ensures that access is granted based on business requirements rather than discretionary user requests. RBAC assigns permissions based on predefined roles, such as "Finance Manager" or "IT Support Specialist," ensuring that users receive only the access necessary for their job functions. ABAC enhances this model by considering additional factors, such as location, device type, security clearance, and business unit. A well-designed ILM policy should incorporate both RBAC and ABAC to enforce least privilege access, preventing excessive permissions and reducing security risks.

Multi-factor authentication (MFA) enforcement should be incorporated into the identity lifecycle policy to enhance security. Organizations should require MFA for all users accessing sensitive data, privileged accounts, or remote applications. Adaptive authentication policies should adjust authentication requirements based on risk signals, ensuring that high-risk login attempts trigger additional verification steps. By enforcing MFA as a standard part of identity lifecycle policies, organizations significantly reduce the likelihood of credential-based attacks and unauthorized access.

Defining identity lifecycle stages and transition rules ensures that identities progress through well-governed phases, from onboarding to role transitions and eventual deprovisioning. Each stage of the identity lifecycle should have clearly defined policies governing account creation, role modifications, access certification, and access revocation. Transition rules should specify conditions under which user roles change, such as job promotions, department transfers, or project assignments. Automating these transitions reduces manual oversight and ensures that access remains aligned with job responsibilities.

Regular access reviews and certifications should be mandatory components of an identity lifecycle policy. Periodic access reviews ensure that users retain only necessary permissions and that inappropriate access is revoked in a timely manner. Organizations should schedule automated access certification campaigns where managers and system owners review and validate user access. Compliance regulations such as GDPR, HIPAA, SOX, and PCI-DSS mandate strict access controls and periodic audits, making access certification a critical requirement for regulatory compliance.

Privileged access management (PAM) integration ensures that highly sensitive accounts, such as administrator and system accounts, follow strict security policies. ILM policies should enforce just-in-time (JIT) privileged access, where users receive elevated permissions only for a limited duration. Privileged accounts should be continuously monitored, with session recording and logging enabled to detect suspicious activity. By incorporating PAM into identity lifecycle policies, organizations reduce the risk of insider threats and prevent the misuse of administrative privileges.

Policy-driven identity synchronization ensures that identity attributes remain consistent across all enterprise systems. Users often have accounts in multiple platforms, including on-premises Active Directory (AD), cloud-based identity providers, and third-party SaaS applications. Without proper synchronization, identity attributes such as job title, department, or email address may become outdated, leading to inconsistencies in access management. ILM policies should enforce real-time identity synchronization across all integrated systems, preventing identity fragmentation and ensuring seamless authentication experiences.

Self-service identity management capabilities improve efficiency while maintaining security. ILM policies should allow users to manage their profiles, reset passwords, and request additional access through self-service portals. Automated approval workflows should route access requests to the appropriate approvers, reducing dependency on IT teams for manual access provisioning. Self-service IAM capabilities enhance user experience, reduce administrative workload, and enable users to resolve identity-related issues independently.

Defining deprovisioning policies and access expiration rules ensures that accounts are properly terminated when users leave the organization or no longer require access. Organizations must enforce immediate access revocation for departing employees and contractors, preventing security risks associated with orphaned accounts. Temporary access should have automatic expiration dates, ensuring that short-term project workers or third-party vendors do not retain unnecessary access. Deprovisioning workflows should extend to non-human identities, such as service accounts and API keys, ensuring that automated processes follow the same security policies as human users.

Continuous monitoring and anomaly detection should be built into identity lifecycle policies to detect unauthorized access attempts, privilege escalation, or identity misuse. AI-driven behavioral analytics can help identify suspicious activities, such as logins from unusual locations, repeated failed authentication attempts, or access requests that deviate from normal patterns. Security teams should leverage SIEM (Security Information and Event Management) integrations to correlate identity-related events with broader security threats, enabling proactive incident response.

Ensuring compliance with industry standards and regulatory frameworks is a fundamental aspect of identity lifecycle policy design. Organizations operating in regulated industries must align ILM policies with standards such as NIST, ISO 27001, CIS Controls, and Zero Trust security frameworks. Regular audits, compliance reporting, and security assessments should be conducted to ensure that ILM policies remain up to date with evolving security and regulatory requirements.

Defining an identity lifecycle governance framework ensures that ILM policies remain adaptable to business changes, emerging security threats, and evolving technology landscapes. Organizations should establish an Identity Governance Board responsible for reviewing and updating ILM policies, conducting risk assessments, and ensuring that identity management practices align with business objectives. Governance frameworks should include incident response plans, ensuring that security teams can quickly respond to identity-related breaches, unauthorized access, or compliance violations.

Implementing best practices in identity lifecycle policy design enables organizations to secure user identities, enforce least privilege access, automate identity workflows, and maintain compliance with industry regulations. By integrating automation, access governance, continuous monitoring, and policy-driven identity synchronization, enterprises build a robust identity lifecycle framework that supports security, operational efficiency, and regulatory compliance.

Identity Federation and Cross-Organization Identity Management

Identity federation and cross-organization identity management enable seamless authentication and access control across multiple enterprises, cloud platforms, and third-party service providers. As organizations expand their digital ecosystems, employees, contractors, business partners, and customers require access to applications and data that span different identity domains. Traditional identity management models, which rely on isolated user directories, create security risks, administrative burdens, and fragmented access experiences. Identity federation provides a standardized approach to enabling single sign-on (SSO) and access control across multiple organizations while maintaining security, compliance, and user convenience.

At the core of identity federation is the concept of trust relationships between identity providers (IdPs) and service providers (SPs). Instead of requiring users to create separate accounts for each organization or service, identity federation allows users to authenticate once with a trusted identity provider and gain access to multiple external applications. This federated authentication model improves user experience, reduces password fatigue, and enhances security by eliminating the need for redundant credentials. Organizations implement federation using protocols such as Security Assertion Markup Language (SAML), OpenID Connect (OIDC), and OAuth 2.0, which enable secure exchange of authentication and authorization data between identity domains.

One of the key benefits of identity federation is enabling seamless authentication across cloud platforms and third-party services. Enterprises increasingly adopt software-as-a-service (SaaS) applications, such as Microsoft 365, Salesforce, and Google Workspace, which require integration with internal IAM systems. Instead of managing separate user credentials for each cloud application, organizations leverage federated identity to extend authentication from their corporate directory, such as Active Directory (AD) or Azure AD, to external services. This approach ensures that users can securely access cloud applications using their existing enterprise credentials, reducing administrative overhead while improving security.

Cross-organization identity management plays a critical role in business-to-business (B2B) collaborations, where employees from different organizations need to access shared resources. Traditional access control mechanisms require organizations to manually create and manage external user accounts, leading to scalability challenges and security risks. Identity federation simplifies B2B access management by enabling partners and vendors to authenticate using their home organization's identity provider. Federated trust models allow organizations to grant access to external users while maintaining centralized control over permissions and security policies.

Just-in-time (JIT) user provisioning enhances cross-organization identity management by dynamically creating user accounts in target applications when external users authenticate for the first time. Instead of pre-provisioning accounts for business partners or third-party vendors, organizations use JIT provisioning to grant access based on authentication claims received from federated identity providers. This approach reduces administrative workload and ensures that external users only receive access when needed. When access is no longer required, federated policies automatically revoke permissions, minimizing security risks associated with orphaned accounts.

Multi-factor authentication (MFA) enforcement across federated environments ensures that authentication remains secure even when users authenticate from external organizations. Identity federation allows organizations to enforce consistent MFA policies, regardless of where authentication originates. If a partner organization does not enforce MFA, the receiving organization can require step-up authentication before granting access to critical resources. Adaptive authentication policies dynamically assess risk levels based on user behavior, device trust, and login context, applying additional verification when necessary.

Privileged access management (PAM) integration with identity federation is essential for securing administrative access in cross-organization environments. Federation extends not only to regular users but also to privileged accounts, which require enhanced security measures. Organizations implement just-in-time (JIT) privileged access, session monitoring, and privileged credential vaulting to ensure that administrative users accessing federated systems follow strict security policies. By integrating PAM with federated identity providers, organizations reduce the risk of privilege escalation attacks and insider threats.

Regulatory compliance and data privacy considerations play a crucial role in cross-organization identity management. Organizations that share identity data across federated environments must comply with regulations such as GDPR, CCPA, HIPAA, and PCI-DSS, ensuring that user credentials and authentication logs are protected. Federated authentication frameworks include identity governance controls, consent management mechanisms, and access logging to ensure compliance with legal requirements. Organizations must define data-sharing agreements and security policies that outline how identity data is processed, stored, and protected across federated environments.

Identity federation in government and public sector collaborations enhances security and interoperability between agencies. Governments implement federated identity frameworks to enable seamless authentication across different departments, ensuring that citizens, government employees, and contractors can securely access shared digital services. Federated authentication standards such as FIDO2, eIDAS, and NIST 800-63 provide guidelines for secure identity management in public-sector environments. By leveraging federated identity, governments reduce administrative complexity, improve security, and enhance the user experience for citizens accessing digital services.

Cross-border identity federation is essential for multinational enterprises that operate in multiple jurisdictions. Employees, partners, and contractors working across different countries need access to global enterprise resources without managing multiple credentials. Organizations implement identity federation with cloud identity providers and regional authentication frameworks, ensuring compliance with local data protection laws while enabling secure global authentication. Federated single sign-on (SSO) simplifies authentication across multinational infrastructures, improving security and operational efficiency.

Decentralized identity and self-sovereign identity (SSI) models are emerging trends in cross-organization identity management. Traditional identity federation relies on centralized identity providers, but decentralized identity models allow users to control their own digital identities using blockchain and distributed ledger technology. Verifiable credentials and decentralized identifiers (DIDs) enable cross-organization authentication without relying on a single authority. While decentralized identity is still evolving, it offers potential benefits for reducing identity fraud, enhancing privacy, and improving cross-border authentication.

Organizations implementing identity federation must establish governance frameworks and trust relationships to ensure security and interoperability. Federated environments require identity trust policies, authentication assurance levels, and security certifications to validate trusted identity providers. Organizations define federation agreements that specify authentication requirements, identity verification standards, and security controls for cross-organization identity management.

Continuous monitoring and identity threat detection are essential for securing federated environments. AI-driven identity analytics and security information and event management (SIEM) solutions help organizations detect suspicious activities, such as unusual login patterns, anomalous access requests, and compromised credentials. Automated identity threat intelligence systems analyze authentication logs and generate alerts when federated authentication anomalies are detected.

Identity federation and cross-organization identity management enable organizations to extend secure authentication beyond their internal boundaries, facilitating seamless access to cloud services, partner ecosystems, and multi-organization collaborations. By implementing standardized authentication protocols, enforcing strong security policies, and integrating with advanced identity governance solutions, organizations enhance security while providing a frictionless user experience. Identity federation is a cornerstone of modern identity management, enabling businesses to securely connect users across distributed digital ecosystems.

Blockchain and Decentralized Identity

Blockchain and decentralized identity are transforming how digital identities are managed, offering a more secure, private, and user-controlled approach to authentication and verification. Traditional identity management models rely on centralized authorities, such as governments, corporations, or identity providers, to issue and validate credentials. While these models provide convenience, they also introduce security risks, such as data breaches, identity theft, and unauthorized surveillance. Blockchain technology introduces a decentralized approach to identity management, allowing individuals to control their own digital identities without relying on a single entity.

Decentralized identity is based on the concept of self-sovereign identity (SSI), which enables users to own and manage their personal identity credentials without needing an intermediary. Unlike traditional identity systems where data is stored in centralized databases, SSI allows individuals to store their identity information in a digital wallet and share it selectively with third parties. Blockchain technology ensures that credentials can be verified in a trustless environment, meaning that no single entity has complete control over the identity verification process. This approach enhances privacy, reduces fraud, and minimizes the risk of unauthorized access to personal data.

Verifiable credentials (VCs) are a key component of decentralized identity systems. VCs are digitally signed identity attestations issued by trusted organizations, such as governments, educational institutions, and financial institutions. For example, a university may issue a verifiable credential to a graduate, proving their degree completion. The graduate can store this credential in their digital wallet and present it to employers without requiring direct contact with the university. Employers can verify the credential using a blockchain-based registry without needing to access a centralized database.

Decentralized identifiers (DIDs) enable individuals and organizations to create and manage their own unique digital identities. Unlike traditional identifiers, such as email addresses or usernames that are controlled by centralized providers, DIDs are generated cryptographically and registered on a blockchain. Each DID is associated with a pair of public and private keys, allowing users to authenticate themselves and sign digital transactions securely. DIDs enhance security by eliminating password-based authentication, reducing the risk of phishing and credential theft.

Blockchain ensures immutability and transparency in identity verification processes. When an identity credential is issued and recorded on a blockchain, it cannot be altered or forged, making it a highly secure method for identity verification. However, personal data is not stored directly on the blockchain to preserve user privacy. Instead, blockchain networks store cryptographic proofs, which validate the authenticity of credentials without exposing sensitive information. This approach complies with privacy regulations such as GDPR and CCPA, ensuring that users retain full control over their personal data.

One of the main use cases of decentralized identity is eliminating password-based authentication. With traditional identity systems, users need to remember multiple passwords for different services, increasing the risk of weak credentials, password reuse, and phishing attacks. Decentralized identity replaces passwords with cryptographic authentication, where users prove their identity using digital signatures. This approach reduces reliance on central authentication servers, making it more resistant to cyberattacks.

In the financial sector, decentralized identity helps combat identity fraud and money laundering. Banks and financial institutions must comply with Know Your Customer (KYC) and Anti-Money Laundering (AML) regulations, which require verifying customer identities before providing services. Decentralized identity allows users to present pre-verified credentials, streamlining the KYC process while reducing costs for financial institutions. By using blockchain-based identity verification, banks can authenticate customers securely without storing large amounts of personally identifiable information (PII) in centralized databases.

Decentralized identity also plays a crucial role in cross-border identity verification. In many countries, individuals struggle to access financial services, healthcare, or government benefits due to a lack of formal identification. Blockchain-based identity solutions enable individuals to obtain portable, verifiable credentials that can be used across different jurisdictions. For example, refugees without official identification documents can receive blockchain-based identity credentials from humanitarian organizations, allowing them to access essential services without needing traditional government-issued IDs.

The healthcare industry benefits from decentralized identity by enabling secure and interoperable patient records. Patients can store their medical history in a decentralized digital wallet and grant temporary access to healthcare providers as needed. This approach ensures that medical records remain private and under the control of the patient, reducing the risk of unauthorized access or data breaches.

Additionally, decentralized identity improves telemedicine authentication, ensuring that only verified healthcare professionals can access sensitive patient data.

One of the challenges of implementing decentralized identity is scalability and interoperability. Multiple blockchain networks and identity frameworks exist, each using different protocols and standards. To achieve widespread adoption, organizations must develop interoperable identity solutions that allow different systems to communicate seamlessly. The Decentralized Identity Foundation (DIF), World Wide Web Consortium (W3C), and Hyperledger Indy are working to establish global standards for decentralized identity to ensure compatibility across various platforms.

Regulatory and legal considerations also impact the adoption of decentralized identity. While blockchain enhances data security and privacy, governments and organizations must ensure that decentralized identity solutions comply with existing identity verification laws and regulations. In some regions, legal frameworks require identity data to be stored within national borders, which can create challenges for blockchain-based identity solutions operating on global networks. Organizations must balance decentralization with compliance, ensuring that regulatory requirements are met while maintaining the core principles of user control and privacy.

Adoption of decentralized identity is expanding across industries, with major technology companies, governments, and financial institutions exploring its potential. Microsoft's Azure AD Verifiable Credentials, IBM's Blockchain Identity, and the European Union's eIDAS framework are leading initiatives in decentralized identity adoption. Governments are piloting blockchain-based digital identity programs to provide citizens with secure, portable identification that can be used for e-government services, financial transactions, and cross-border travel.

Blockchain and decentralized identity offer a transformative approach to digital identity management, providing enhanced security, privacy, and user control. By eliminating centralized identity repositories, reducing reliance on passwords, and enabling verifiable digital credentials, decentralized identity systems pave the way for a more secure and privacy-centric digital ecosystem. As adoption grows and standards mature, decentralized identity is set to redefine how individuals and organizations interact in the digital world.

Machine Learning in Identity Lifecycle Management

Machine learning is transforming identity lifecycle management by enhancing automation, improving security, and optimizing access control decisions. Traditional identity management relies on static policies, predefined rules, and manual interventions to create, modify, and deactivate user accounts. However, as IT environments become more complex and cyber threats grow more sophisticated, machine learning enables organizations to make data-driven identity decisions, detect anomalies, and improve governance. By leveraging artificial intelligence (AI) and machine learning, identity lifecycle management becomes more adaptive, proactive, and secure.

One of the key areas where machine learning enhances identity lifecycle management is user behavior analysis. Organizations generate vast amounts of identity-related data, including login attempts, access requests, role changes, and authentication failures. Machine learning models analyze this data to establish normal behavioral patterns for each user. When deviations from normal behavior occur, such as an employee logging in from an unusual location or accessing a system they have never used before, machine learning algorithms can flag the activity as suspicious and trigger additional security measures. This approach helps detect unauthorized access attempts, compromised credentials, and insider threats.

Automated user provisioning and role assignment is another major benefit of machine learning in identity lifecycle management. Traditionally, organizations assign user roles based on predefined job functions, requiring IT teams to manually adjust permissions as employees change positions. Machine learning optimizes this process by analyzing historical access patterns, job roles, and peer group behaviors to recommend appropriate access levels. When a new employee joins the organization, AI-powered IAM systems can predict which applications and permissions they need based on similar user profiles, reducing administrative workload and ensuring least privilege access.

Machine learning enhances identity risk assessment by analyzing multiple risk factors in real time. Traditional IAM systems rely on static access control lists, which do not account for contextual risk signals, such as device reputation, login frequency, and past authentication failures. Machine learning models process these signals to calculate a dynamic risk score for each access attempt. If an authentication request is deemed high risk—such as a login from an unrecognized device or a country with high cybercrime activity—the system can enforce adaptive authentication, requiring additional verification steps before granting access.

Privileged access management (PAM) security benefits significantly from machine learning, as privileged accounts pose a high risk if misused or compromised. AI-powered IAM solutions monitor privileged users' behavior, comparing current activities with historical patterns to detect unusual privilege escalations or unauthorized system modifications. For example, if an administrator suddenly accesses critical databases outside normal working hours or modifies security configurations without prior approvals, machine learning algorithms can generate alerts, restrict access, or trigger session monitoring. By continuously analyzing privileged user behavior, machine learning strengthens security and prevents privilege abuse.

Machine learning also plays a crucial role in identity reconciliation and data synchronization across hybrid IT environments. Organizations manage identities across multiple directories, cloud applications, and legacy systems, often leading to data inconsistencies. Machine learning algorithms detect mismatches between identity attributes, helping organizations identify orphaned accounts, duplicate identities, and outdated permissions. By automatically reconciling identity records, AI-driven IAM solutions improve data integrity and reduce security risks associated with misconfigured access rights.

Anomaly detection in authentication and access requests is another area where machine learning enhances security. By continuously learning from historical access patterns, AI-driven IAM platforms can detect login anomalies, suspicious access behaviors, and unauthorized data transfers. If an employee's access request deviates significantly from their usual behavior, machine learning models can trigger automated security responses, such as requiring additional authentication, notifying security teams, or revoking access temporarily. This proactive approach helps prevent identity-based attacks, including credential stuffing, brute force attacks, and phishing attempts.

Machine learning-driven continuous access reviews streamline compliance efforts by automating the process of certifying user access. Traditional access review processes require managers to manually verify whether employees still need their assigned permissions, leading to inefficiencies and compliance gaps. Machine learning simplifies this process by identifying low-risk and high-risk access scenarios. For example, users who consistently access approved systems without anomalies may require fewer manual reviews, while users with irregular access behaviors can be prioritized for review. This targeted approach reduces compliance workload while ensuring that only necessary permissions are retained.

AI-powered IAM solutions improve self-service identity management by enabling conversational AI chatbots and automated helpdesk functions. Employees often need assistance with password resets, access requests, and multi-factor authentication setup. Machine learning enhances self-service IAM portals by understanding user queries, predicting common issues, and providing automated solutions. For instance, AI chatbots can guide users through password recovery steps, recommend access approvals based on historical requests, and automate identity verification for self-service onboarding. This reduces IT support ticket volume and improves user experience.

Machine learning contributes to fraud detection and identity proofing by analyzing identity verification attempts in real time. Organizations that require strong identity proofing mechanisms, such as banks, healthcare providers, and government agencies, use AI to detect forged documents, synthetic identities, and impersonation attempts. AI-powered facial recognition, biometric authentication, and document analysis tools compare real-time identity verification data with historical records to detect inconsistencies. By preventing fraudulent identity creation, machine learning strengthens security in customer identity and access management (CIAM).

The integration of machine learning with zero trust security models enhances identity lifecycle management by continuously verifying users and enforcing context-aware access controls. Zero trust principles require continuous authentication and real-time risk assessment, rather than granting permanent trust based on a single login session. Machine learning helps enforce zero trust by dynamically adjusting access policies based on evolving risk levels. If an employee who usually works from the United States suddenly logs in from an unverified device in another country, AI-driven IAM systems can require step-up authentication or block the request entirely.

Machine learning also enables predictive identity analytics, helping organizations forecast identity-related risks before they become security incidents. AI models analyze patterns such as failed login attempts, excessive privilege requests, and dormant accounts to predict potential security threats. If a system detects a sudden increase in access requests to sensitive files, it can proactively investigate potential insider threats or compromised accounts. By leveraging predictive analytics, organizations improve their ability to anticipate and mitigate identity-related security risks.

As machine learning continues to evolve, its impact on identity lifecycle management will grow, making IAM systems more intelligent, efficient, and secure. By automating identity governance, enhancing risk-based authentication, and improving access decision-making, machine learning transforms how organizations manage identities, detect threats, and enforce security policies.

Cybersecurity Threats and Identity Risks

Cybersecurity threats targeting digital identities have increased in frequency and sophistication, posing significant risks to organizations and individuals. As businesses adopt cloud services, remote work environments, and interconnected digital platforms, identity has become a primary target for cybercriminals seeking unauthorized access to sensitive data and systems. Weak identity security measures expose organizations to financial losses, reputational damage, and regulatory penalties. Understanding cybersecurity threats and identity risks is essential for implementing robust identity and access management (IAM) strategies to protect users, systems, and data.

One of the most prevalent identity-related threats is credential theft, where attackers steal usernames and passwords to gain unauthorized access to accounts. Cybercriminals use methods such as phishing, credential stuffing, and keylogging to harvest login credentials. Phishing attacks trick users into providing their credentials through fraudulent emails, fake websites, or social engineering tactics. Credential stuffing exploits reused or leaked passwords by attempting large-scale automated login attempts across multiple platforms. Keylogging malware secretly records keystrokes to capture sensitive login information. Organizations combat credential theft by enforcing multi-factor authentication (MFA), password policies, and security awareness training.

Account takeover (ATO) attacks occur when cybercriminals successfully compromise user accounts using stolen credentials. Once inside an account, attackers can access confidential data, modify permissions, and execute fraudulent transactions. In financial services, ATO attacks lead to unauthorized fund transfers, while in enterprise environments, they facilitate insider threats and data breaches. Attackers often evade detection by mimicking legitimate user behavior, making ATOs difficult to identify. AI-driven behavioral analytics help detect anomalies in login patterns and trigger security responses when suspicious activities occur.

Insider threats pose another significant identity risk, as employees, contractors, or business partners with access to sensitive systems may intentionally or unintentionally expose data. Malicious insiders misuse their privileges for financial gain, corporate espionage, or personal grievances. Accidental insider threats occur when employees mishandle data, misconfigure security settings, or fall victim to phishing attacks. Organizations mitigate insider threats through least privilege access, real-time activity monitoring, and privileged access management (PAM) solutions that restrict excessive permissions and enforce accountability.

Session hijacking and token theft involve cybercriminals intercepting authentication sessions to impersonate legitimate users. Attackers exploit session cookies, OAuth tokens, and API keys to bypass authentication mechanisms. Techniques such as man-in-the-middle (MITM) attacks and session replay attacks allow attackers to steal active session tokens, gaining unauthorized access to systems without requiring credentials. Secure session management policies, token expiration controls, and encrypted communications help prevent session hijacking risks.

Ransomware and identity-based attacks have evolved to target privileged accounts and enterprise IAM systems. Ransomware operators gain initial access through compromised credentials, phishing emails, or remote desktop protocol (RDP) vulnerabilities. Once inside the network, attackers escalate privileges, disable security tools, and encrypt critical data, demanding ransom payments. Identity protection measures such as zero trust security frameworks, network segmentation, and real-time identity threat detection are essential for preventing ransomware incidents.

Business email compromise (BEC) and executive impersonation attacks exploit digital identities to deceive employees into making fraudulent transactions or sharing confidential information. Attackers impersonate executives, vendors, or business partners using spoofed email domains and social engineering techniques. BEC attacks often bypass traditional spam filters, relying on psychological manipulation rather than malicious links or attachments. Organizations implement email authentication protocols (DMARC, SPF, and DKIM), user verification procedures, and AI-based fraud detection to counteract BEC threats.

Identity fraud and synthetic identity attacks involve creating fraudulent digital identities using a combination of real and fabricated information. Cybercriminals use stolen personal data from data breaches to construct synthetic identities that pass identity verification checks. These fake identities are then used for financial fraud, credit card scams, and fraudulent account openings. AI-powered identity verification solutions analyze user behavior, document authenticity, and biometric patterns to detect synthetic identities and prevent fraud.

API security vulnerabilities present a growing identity risk, as organizations rely on application programming interfaces (APIs) for authentication, data exchange, and cloud service integrations. Poorly secured APIs allow attackers to exploit authentication flaws, extract sensitive data, and manipulate identity records. API security best practices include OAuth 2.0 token validation, role-based API access control, and API threat monitoring to prevent unauthorized access and data leaks.

Shadow IT and unauthorized identity management occur when employees use unapproved cloud applications and personal devices for work-related tasks. Shadow IT creates identity visibility gaps, where IT teams lack oversight of user accounts, authentication methods, and access permissions across unmonitored platforms. Organizations address shadow IT risks by implementing cloud access security brokers (CASBs), identity governance policies, and automated application discovery tools to ensure all digital identities are managed securely.

Deepfake technology and biometric identity spoofing introduce new threats to identity verification processes. Deepfake AI generates realistic voice and facial replicas that can bypass biometric authentication systems. Attackers use deepfake technology to impersonate executives, bypass facial recognition controls, and manipulate video verification processes. Organizations combat deepfake threats with liveness detection, AI-driven facial recognition security, and multi-modal biometric authentication that combines multiple identity verification factors.

Supply chain and third-party identity risks arise when external vendors, contractors, and service providers have access to enterprise systems. Organizations often struggle to enforce consistent identity security policies across third-party integrations, leading to increased attack surfaces. Cybercriminals target weak identity controls in supply chain networks to compromise credentials, infiltrate enterprise networks, and launch supply chain attacks. Secure third-party identity management requires federated identity solutions, risk-based authentication, and continuous monitoring of vendor access.

Zero trust security models and identity-based threat prevention provide a modern approach to mitigating identity risks. Unlike traditional perimeter-based security models, zero trust enforces continuous authentication, least privilege access, and micro-segmentation to prevent unauthorized access. Zero trust IAM solutions incorporate risk-based authentication (RBA), just-in-time (JIT) access provisioning, and machine learning-driven anomaly detection to dynamically assess and respond to identity threats in real time.

Organizations must adopt proactive identity security measures to defend against evolving cyber threats targeting digital identities. By integrating multi-factor authentication, AI-driven behavioral analytics, privileged access controls, and real-time identity monitoring, businesses can enhance identity security, reduce attack surfaces, and prevent unauthorized access to critical systems. Cybersecurity threats will continue to evolve, making identity-centric security frameworks essential for protecting digital assets, user credentials, and enterprise data.

Incident Response and Identity Breach Management

Incident response and identity breach management are critical components of an organization's cybersecurity strategy, ensuring that identity-related security incidents are detected, contained, and mitigated effectively. As digital identities become prime targets for cybercriminals, organizations must implement robust incident response frameworks to minimize the impact of identity breaches, protect sensitive data, and restore normal operations. A well-defined incident response plan enables organizations to respond swiftly to threats, limit financial and reputational damage, and comply with regulatory requirements.

The first phase of identity breach management is incident detection and identification. Security teams must continuously monitor authentication logs, access patterns, and privileged account activities to detect signs of unauthorized access. Machine learning and AI-driven security analytics enhance detection capabilities by identifying anomalous login behavior, unauthorized privilege escalations, and credential misuse. Organizations integrate Security Information and Event Management (SIEM) systems, User and Entity Behavior

Analytics (UEBA), and real-time identity threat detection tools to identify potential breaches before they escalate.

Once an identity-related security incident is detected, the next step is incident classification and risk assessment. Security teams evaluate the severity of the breach by determining the scope of the compromise, affected identities, and potential data exposure. Incidents are classified based on their impact, such as unauthorized access to sensitive systems, compromised administrator accounts, or leaked personally identifiable information (PII). The classification process helps organizations prioritize response actions, allocate resources effectively, and determine whether regulatory notifications are required.

Containment and mitigation are crucial for limiting the spread of an identity breach. Immediate actions include disabling compromised accounts, revoking active session tokens, enforcing step-up authentication, and blocking malicious IP addresses. Organizations implement automated identity threat response mechanisms, where AI-driven security tools quarantine suspicious user accounts, require password resets, and enforce temporary account lockdowns to prevent further unauthorized access. For breaches involving privileged accounts, privileged session termination, emergency credential rotation, and temporary access restrictions are enforced to contain the threat.

Forensic analysis and root cause investigation help security teams understand how the breach occurred, identify vulnerabilities, and prevent future incidents. Security analysts examine authentication logs, access control changes, API request history, and external login attempts to trace the attacker's movements and determine the initial point of compromise. If stolen credentials were used, analysts assess whether they were obtained from phishing attacks, password reuse, or credential stuffing attempts. Organizations leverage cyber threat intelligence (CTI) feeds, dark web monitoring, and breach notification services to track compromised identity data and prevent reuse in future attacks.

Regulatory compliance plays a significant role in identity breach management. Organizations handling sensitive data must adhere to regulations such as GDPR, HIPAA, CCPA, and PCI-DSS, which mandate timely breach notifications, incident reporting, and data protection measures. Depending on the severity of the breach, organizations may be required to inform affected users, report incidents to regulatory authorities, and implement corrective actions to enhance identity security. Failure to comply with breach notification laws can result in legal penalties, fines, and reputational damage.

Communication and user notification are critical in maintaining transparency and trust after an identity breach. Affected individuals must be informed promptly, with clear instructions on how to reset passwords, enable multi-factor authentication (MFA), and monitor their accounts for suspicious activity. Organizations provide secure breach notification channels, ensuring that phishing attempts disguised as breach alerts do not further exploit affected users. Security teams issue incident advisories, FAQs, and cybersecurity awareness guidance to help users protect their identities and prevent account takeovers.

Following containment and mitigation, organizations must implement long-term remediation measures to strengthen identity security. Security teams conduct post-incident security assessments, patch identity management vulnerabilities, and enhance authentication controls to prevent recurrence. Organizations enforce identity lifecycle management best practices, implement just-in-time (JIT) access provisioning, and integrate behavioral analytics for continuous identity monitoring.

Privileged access review and remediation is a key aspect of post-breach identity security. Security teams audit privileged accounts, enforce role-based access control (RBAC), and conduct periodic access reviews to identify excessive privileges and remove unnecessary access. Temporary elevated privileges granted during the incident response phase are revoked, and privileged access management (PAM) controls are reinforced to prevent privilege escalation attacks.

Password policies and credential security must be reassessed following an identity breach. Organizations enforce password rotation for affected accounts, prevent the reuse of compromised credentials, and implement passwordless authentication methods to enhance security. Dark web monitoring tools track leaked credentials and exposed identity data, alerting security teams if breached accounts resurface in underground markets.

Identity security awareness training helps employees and users recognize identity threats, improve password hygiene, and avoid social engineering attacks. Organizations conduct regular phishing simulations, MFA adoption campaigns, and zero trust security awareness programs to reduce human error in identity breaches. Employees are trained to identify suspicious login attempts, unauthorized access alerts, and account takeover risks, enabling them to report potential threats proactively.

Organizations adopt zero trust security principles to prevent future identity breaches by implementing continuous authentication, least privilege access, and micro-segmentation. Unlike traditional perimeter-based security models, zero trust enforces real-time identity verification, dynamic access policies, and risk-based authentication controls to mitigate identity threats. AI-driven risk scoring mechanisms evaluate user behavior, device trust, and access context to detect and prevent unauthorized access attempts.

Post-incident reporting and lessons learned enable organizations to refine their identity breach response strategies. Security teams document incident timelines, response effectiveness, and security control gaps, ensuring that future breaches are managed more efficiently. Post-incident audits help organizations identify areas for improvement in IAM systems, security policies, and breach detection mechanisms.

Cybersecurity teams integrate automated threat response workflows with IAM solutions to enhance real-time incident detection, automated remediation, and risk-based access controls. Organizations deploy SIEM and Security Orchestration, Automation, and Response (SOAR) solutions to orchestrate identity security responses, correlating breach indicators with broader cybersecurity threats.

By implementing a proactive identity breach response framework, organizations enhance their resilience against identity-related cyberattacks, protect user identities, and ensure compliance with regulatory mandates. Strengthening identity security, enforcing adaptive authentication, and leveraging AI-driven threat detection enables organizations to detect, contain, and mitigate identity breaches effectively, reducing the long-term impact of security incidents.

Managing Identity for IoT and Smart Devices

The rapid expansion of the Internet of Things (IoT) has introduced new challenges in identity management, as billions of connected devices require authentication, access control, and lifecycle management. Unlike traditional user identities, IoT devices often operate autonomously, exchanging data and performing critical functions without direct human intervention. Managing identity for IoT and smart devices involves securing device authentication, enforcing access policies, and ensuring that identities remain protected throughout the device lifecycle.

One of the primary challenges in IoT identity management is device authentication. Unlike human users who authenticate using passwords or biometrics, IoT devices require secure authentication mechanisms that do not rely on traditional login credentials. Organizations implement certificate-based authentication, hardware security modules (HSMs), and cryptographic key management to verify device identities. Public Key Infrastructure (PKI) provides a scalable solution for issuing and managing digital certificates, allowing devices to authenticate securely without exposing credentials to attackers.

Unique device identity assignment is essential for managing large-scale IoT networks. Each connected device must have a distinct identity that enables authentication, authorization, and tracking. Organizations generate device identity attributes, such as UUIDs (Universally Unique Identifiers), MAC addresses, and cryptographic fingerprints, ensuring that each device can be uniquely identified within an IoT ecosystem. Without proper identity assignment, attackers can impersonate devices, intercept data, and manipulate network communications.

Identity federation and cross-platform authentication enable IoT devices to interact securely across different environments, including cloud platforms, industrial control systems, and edge computing networks. Federated identity models allow devices to authenticate seamlessly between IoT service providers, enterprise networks, and third-party applications. Organizations implement OAuth 2.0, OpenID Connect (OIDC), and device attestation protocols to extend identity trust across interconnected ecosystems.

Zero Trust security principles play a critical role in IoT identity management, ensuring that no device is inherently trusted. Traditional security models assume that once a device is authenticated, it can communicate freely within the network. However, IoT security frameworks enforce continuous authentication, least privilege access, and dynamic policy enforcement to restrict device interactions based on risk factors. If an IoT device behaves abnormally—such as attempting unauthorized data transfers or communicating with untrusted networks—zero trust policies trigger access restrictions or require re-authentication.

Lifecycle identity management for IoT devices ensures that device identities are created, maintained, and revoked as needed. The IoT lifecycle consists of provisioning, active operation, maintenance, and decommissioning, each requiring strict identity controls. When a device is first introduced into a network, identity provisioning assigns it a unique identifier and enforces authentication policies. Throughout its operational life, identity governance frameworks monitor device behavior, detect anomalies, and update security credentials to prevent unauthorized access. When a device reaches the end of its lifecycle, deprovisioning processes remove its identity credentials, ensuring that it cannot be exploited for malicious purposes.

Machine-to-Machine (M2M) authentication enhances IoT security by allowing devices to communicate securely without human intervention. In industrial IoT environments, autonomous systems such as robotic process automation (RPA), self-driving vehicles, and smart sensors rely on M2M authentication to exchange encrypted messages. Organizations use mutual authentication protocols, digital certificates, and hardware-based security to prevent unauthorized devices from participating in critical system operations.

Edge computing and decentralized identity management are transforming how IoT devices authenticate in distributed networks. Traditional IoT architectures rely on centralized identity management systems, which may introduce latency and single points of failure. Edge computing shifts authentication processes closer to the device, enabling real-time identity verification at the network's edge. Blockchain-based decentralized identity (DID) models allow IoT devices to maintain self-sovereign identities, reducing dependency on central authentication authorities.

IoT identity governance and access control enforce security policies that define what devices can access, what data they can transmit, and how they interact with other systems. Organizations implement role-based access control (RBAC) and attribute-based access control (ABAC) to restrict device permissions based on predefined policies. For example, a medical IoT device used in a hospital may only communicate with authorized healthcare systems, preventing unauthorized access to patient data.

API security for IoT identity management ensures that devices authenticate securely when interacting with cloud platforms, mobile applications, and third-party services. IoT devices often expose RESTful APIs, MQTT protocols, and WebSockets for data transmission, making them susceptible to API-based attacks. Organizations use OAuth 2.0 authorization flows, API gateways, and secure token exchange mechanisms to validate device identities and prevent unauthorized API access.

Device identity monitoring and anomaly detection provide continuous visibility into IoT authentication events. AI-driven identity analytics detect suspicious login attempts, privilege escalation, and abnormal device behavior, allowing security teams to respond in real time. If an IoT device starts exhibiting unusual traffic patterns, such as connecting to unauthorized servers or attempting excessive authentication requests, automated threat response mechanisms isolate the device, revoke its credentials, and initiate forensic investigations.

Firmware and identity security updates are crucial for protecting IoT identities against evolving cyber threats. Attackers exploit outdated device firmware to bypass authentication mechanisms and gain control over IoT networks. Organizations enforce secure firmware updates, over-the-air (OTA) patching, and cryptographic integrity checks to ensure that IoT devices maintain strong identity security throughout their lifecycle.

Regulatory compliance for IoT identity management requires organizations to implement strong authentication and identity governance frameworks. IoT security regulations, such as GDPR, NIST 800-183, and IoT Cybersecurity Improvement Act, mandate that connected devices follow strict identity protection measures. Compliance frameworks enforce secure identity provisioning, encrypted authentication channels, and auditable access logs to mitigate identity-related threats in IoT ecosystems.

As IoT adoption continues to expand across industries, securing device identities becomes a fundamental requirement for maintaining network integrity, preventing cyber threats, and ensuring data privacy. Organizations that implement strong authentication, lifecycle identity governance, and continuous security monitoring enhance the resilience of their IoT infrastructures while mitigating risks associated with identity spoofing, unauthorized device access, and machine-to-machine security breaches.

Future Trends in Identity and Access Management

Identity and access management (IAM) is evolving rapidly as organizations adapt to emerging cybersecurity threats, regulatory requirements, and digital transformation initiatives. Traditional IAM models, which rely on static authentication and role-based access controls, are becoming insufficient in a landscape where cloud computing, hybrid work environments, and interconnected digital services demand more advanced identity security solutions. Future trends in IAM focus on improving security, enhancing user experience, and leveraging artificial intelligence (AI) to enable dynamic, context-aware identity management.

One of the most significant trends in IAM is the shift towards passwordless authentication. Traditional passwords remain one of the weakest links in security, as users often reuse credentials, fall victim to phishing attacks, or create weak passwords that are easy to compromise. Passwordless authentication replaces passwords with more secure alternatives, such as biometric authentication, hardware security keys, cryptographic tokens, and passkeys. The adoption of Fast Identity Online (FIDO2) standards enables passwordless authentication across websites and enterprise systems, reducing the risk of credential-based attacks and improving user experience.

Decentralized identity and self-sovereign identity (SSI) are gaining momentum as organizations explore blockchain-based authentication models. Traditional IAM systems rely on centralized identity providers, which create single points of failure and privacy concerns. Decentralized identity solutions allow users to control their own digital identities using verifiable credentials (VCs) and decentralized identifiers (DIDs) stored in secure digital wallets. Blockchain technology ensures that identities are tamper-proof and verifiable without relying on a central authority. This model enhances privacy, reduces the risk of identity theft, and empowers users to share only the necessary identity attributes with third parties.

Zero Trust security models are becoming the standard approach for identity and access management. Unlike traditional perimeter-based security, Zero Trust assumes that no user, device, or application should be inherently trusted. IAM solutions are integrating Zero Trust principles by enforcing continuous authentication, least privilege access, and real-time risk assessments. Adaptive access controls analyze contextual factors such as device health, geolocation, network security posture, and behavioral biometrics to determine whether a user should be granted access. Organizations implement risk-based authentication (RBA) to dynamically adjust security requirements based on real-time risk levels.

AI-driven identity analytics and behavioral biometrics are transforming how organizations manage access control. Traditional IAM systems rely on static rules and role-based access control (RBAC), which can be ineffective against modern threats. AI-powered IAM platforms analyze user behavior, login patterns, and device interactions to detect anomalies and identify potential security risks. Behavioral biometrics track keystroke dynamics, mouse movements, and navigation habits to create unique user profiles, making it harder for attackers to impersonate legitimate users. AI-driven anomaly detection enables organizations to respond to identity threats proactively, reducing the risk of account takeovers and insider threats.

Federated identity management and cross-organization authentication are becoming essential as businesses collaborate across multiple digital ecosystems. Organizations increasingly rely on third-party applications, cloud services, and partner networks, requiring seamless and secure authentication mechanisms. Federated identity protocols, such as OAuth 2.0, OpenID Connect (OIDC), and SAML, allow users to authenticate across multiple platforms using a single set of credentials. This reduces login friction, improves user convenience, and minimizes security vulnerabilities associated with credential reuse. The rise of verifiable credentials and decentralized identity models further enhances federated authentication by enabling secure, portable digital identities across different organizations.

Identity orchestration and automation are becoming critical for managing complex IAM environments. Organizations are adopting identity-as-a-service (IDaaS) solutions that provide centralized identity management capabilities across cloud, hybrid, and multi-cloud environments. Identity orchestration platforms automate provisioning, deprovisioning, access approvals, and compliance reporting, reducing administrative overhead and improving security. AI-driven identity governance solutions help organizations detect orphaned accounts, enforce least privilege access, and streamline identity compliance processes. Automated IAM workflows enhance operational efficiency while minimizing human errors in identity administration.

The convergence of IAM and cybersecurity is driving the integration of IAM solutions with Security Information and Event Management (SIEM), Endpoint Detection and Response (EDR), and Security Orchestration, Automation, and Response (SOAR) platforms. Traditional IAM solutions focused primarily on authentication and authorization, but modern identity security strategies extend to continuous monitoring, threat detection, and automated incident response. By integrating IAM with cybersecurity frameworks, organizations can correlate identity-related security events with broader attack patterns, enhancing threat visibility and incident response capabilities.

Identity management for the Internet of Things (IoT) and smart devices is becoming a growing concern as connected devices proliferate across industries. Unlike traditional IAM, which focuses on human users, IoT identity management must authenticate machines, sensors, and autonomous systems securely. Organizations implement certificate-based authentication, device attestation, and machine-to-machine (M2M) identity verification to ensure that only authorized devices can communicate within an IoT network. AI-powered IAM solutions help detect anomalous device behavior, revoke compromised device credentials, and enforce Zero Trust policies for IoT identity security.

Regulatory compliance and identity governance are driving the adoption of advanced IAM frameworks that align with privacy laws and security mandates. Regulations such as GDPR, CCPA, PSD2, HIPAA, and NIST 800-63 require organizations to implement strict identity verification, access control, and data protection measures. IAM solutions are incorporating automated compliance reporting, access certification workflows, and privacy-preserving authentication to help businesses meet regulatory requirements. Consent management and data minimization practices ensure that user identities are protected while maintaining compliance with global privacy standards.

Digital identity verification and fraud prevention are becoming increasingly important as businesses move to online-first models. Financial services, healthcare, and e-commerce organizations require strong identity proofing mechanisms to prevent fraud, identity theft, and synthetic identity creation. AI-driven identity verification solutions analyze biometric data, document authenticity, and device reputation to validate users. Organizations use liveness detection, facial recognition, and real-time risk scoring to detect fraudulent identity attempts and prevent unauthorized account openings.

The rise of quantum computing and its impact on identity security is an emerging challenge for IAM. Quantum computers have the potential to break traditional cryptographic algorithms, making many existing authentication and encryption methods obsolete.

Organizations are preparing for a post-quantum cryptography era by adopting quantum-resistant encryption algorithms, secure key exchange protocols, and next-generation cryptographic identity verification methods. IAM vendors are integrating quantum-safe security measures to future-proof identity management against evolving cryptographic threats.

As IAM continues to evolve, organizations must embrace AI-driven automation, decentralized identity models, and Zero Trust security frameworks to stay ahead of cyber threats and compliance challenges. Future IAM solutions will focus on seamless user experiences, adaptive security policies, and intelligent threat detection, ensuring that identity remains the foundation of digital security. By adopting these emerging trends, businesses can enhance identity protection, streamline access control, and build resilient cybersecurity strategies in an increasingly interconnected digital world.

Identity Lifecycle in the Age of AI and Automation

The rise of artificial intelligence (AI) and automation is transforming identity lifecycle management, reshaping how organizations create, manage, and secure digital identities. Traditional identity lifecycle processes relied on manual workflows, predefined policies, and human oversight to provision, modify, and revoke access for users. However, as IT environments become more complex and cyber threats grow more sophisticated, AI-driven automation is revolutionizing identity and access management (IAM) by improving efficiency, reducing errors, and enhancing security. Organizations are now leveraging machine learning, robotic process automation (RPA), and AI-driven analytics to streamline identity governance and enforce adaptive access controls.

One of the key advantages of AI in identity lifecycle management is automated identity provisioning and deprovisioning. In the past, IT teams manually created user accounts, assigned roles, and granted access based on job functions. This process was time-consuming, prone to human error, and often led to delays in onboarding new employees. AI-driven IAM platforms analyze historical access patterns, organizational structures, and peer group behaviors to automatically provision access based on contextual insights. When an employee joins an organization, AI-based systems can predict the necessary applications, security groups, and privileges required for their role, reducing administrative workload and improving user productivity.

AI-driven dynamic role management enhances identity lifecycle automation by continuously adjusting access permissions based on real-time data. Traditional role-based access control (RBAC) models rely on static roles that do not adapt to changing job functions or evolving security risks. AI-powered IAM solutions dynamically adjust role assignments based on machine learning algorithms, risk assessments, and behavioral analytics. If an employee transitions to a new department, AI automatically modifies their access rights, ensuring that they receive the necessary permissions while removing outdated access that could pose security risks.

Risk-based authentication and adaptive access control are critical advancements in AI-driven identity management. Instead of applying uniform authentication policies for all users, AI enables context-aware authentication, adjusting security requirements based on real-time risk factors. AI models analyze factors such as user location, device trust, login patterns, and network security posture to determine the level of authentication required. If an employee logs in from a trusted device at their usual location, they may receive frictionless authentication. However, if an access request originates from an unfamiliar location or a high-risk device, AI can enforce multi-factor authentication (MFA), biometric verification, or temporary access restrictions.

The integration of machine learning-driven anomaly detection strengthens security by identifying irregular access behaviors and insider threats. AI continuously monitors identity activities, detecting deviations from normal behavior that may indicate compromised credentials, unauthorized access, or privilege escalation attacks. If an employee suddenly requests access to sensitive financial data or logs in from multiple locations within a short timeframe, AI-driven IAM systems trigger real-time security alerts, automated access revocation, or risk-based authentication challenges. This proactive approach reduces the time required to detect and respond to identity-related security incidents.

AI-enhanced identity governance and compliance streamline regulatory compliance by automating access reviews, audit reporting, and policy enforcement. Organizations must comply with industry regulations such as GDPR, HIPAA, PCI-DSS, and SOX, which require strict identity controls and periodic access certifications. AI automates compliance processes by identifying orphaned accounts, excessive privileges, and unauthorized access rights, ensuring that organizations maintain least privilege access and enforce identity governance policies effectively. AI-driven compliance dashboards provide real-time visibility into identity risks, helping security teams identify potential violations before they lead to regulatory penalties.

The adoption of robotic process automation (RPA) for identity lifecycle management further enhances efficiency by automating repetitive IAM tasks. RPA bots perform actions such as password resets, access requests, identity synchronization, and privilege adjustments without requiring manual intervention. In large organizations, RPA streamlines onboarding and offboarding processes, ensuring that user accounts are created, modified, or deactivated in real time based on HR system updates. By reducing manual IAM workloads, RPA allows IT teams to focus on strategic security initiatives while improving operational efficiency.

AI-powered self-service IAM portals empower users to manage their identities securely while reducing reliance on IT support. Traditional IAM systems required users to submit manual requests for password resets, account unlocks, and access approvals, leading to delays and increased helpdesk costs. AI-driven chatbots and virtual assistants now provide automated identity assistance, guiding users through identity verification processes, password recovery, and access management workflows. By integrating natural language processing (NLP) and AI-driven decision-making, self-service IAM solutions improve user experience while enhancing security controls.

The role of AI in privileged access management (PAM) is becoming increasingly important as organizations seek to protect high-risk administrative accounts. AI-driven PAM solutions continuously monitor privileged user activities, detecting unusual privilege escalations, unauthorized administrative actions, and suspicious session behaviors. If AI identifies an anomaly—such as a privileged user accessing sensitive databases outside business hours—it can automatically enforce just-in-time (JIT) privileged access restrictions, revoke administrative credentials, or require step-up authentication. By applying AI to PAM, organizations strengthen security for critical IT infrastructure while reducing the risk of insider threats and credential-based attacks.

Identity lifecycle automation for non-human identities is an emerging trend in IAM. As organizations deploy IoT devices, cloud workloads, and API-based services, managing non-human identities becomes a security challenge. AI-driven identity management solutions automatically generate machine-to-machine (M2M) credentials, enforce API security policies, and detect compromised service accounts. AI monitors device authentication patterns, API interactions, and cloud service permissions, identifying potential identity threats before they are exploited. Automated identity lifecycle management ensures that machine identities are properly provisioned, monitored, and revoked when no longer needed.

AI-driven fraud prevention and identity proofing enhance identity verification processes for customer identity and access management (CIAM). Businesses require strong identity verification to prevent account takeovers, synthetic identity fraud, and social engineering attacks. AI-powered identity proofing solutions analyze biometric authentication data, document authenticity, and behavioral risk signals to verify customer identities accurately. AI also detects deepfake fraud, identity spoofing, and credential stuffing attacks, ensuring that only legitimate users gain access to digital services.

As AI and automation continue to reshape IAM, organizations are adopting Zero Trust security architectures that enforce continuous identity verification, real-time access monitoring, and risk-based authentication. AI-driven IAM solutions integrate with cloud security platforms, endpoint protection systems, and security orchestration tools to provide a holistic approach to identity security.

By leveraging AI-driven automation, machine learning analytics, and robotic process automation, identity lifecycle management evolves into an adaptive, intelligent, and security-first framework. These advancements enable organizations to enhance security, improve user experience, and streamline compliance while reducing administrative overhead and minimizing identity-related risks. AI and automation will continue to drive the future of IAM, ensuring that identity security remains a foundational pillar of digital transformation and cybersecurity strategies.

Ethical Considerations in Identity Management

Identity management plays a crucial role in securing digital interactions, protecting sensitive information, and enabling trusted access to systems and services. However, as identity and access management (IAM) technologies evolve, ethical concerns surrounding data privacy, consent, bias, and surveillance become increasingly important. Organizations must balance security and user convenience while ensuring that identity management practices respect fundamental human rights and align with ethical standards. The ethical challenges in identity management require organizations to implement transparent policies, prioritize user control, and mitigate risks associated with identity misuse.

One of the most significant ethical concerns in identity management is data privacy and user consent. Digital identities contain personal and sensitive information, including biometric data, authentication credentials, and behavioral patterns. Organizations collecting and storing this data must ensure that individuals have control over how their identities are managed and shared. Privacy laws such as the General Data Protection Regulation (GDPR), California Consumer Privacy Act (CCPA), and other data protection frameworks emphasize the importance of obtaining user consent before processing personal data. Ethical identity management requires organizations to provide clear, informed consent mechanisms, allowing users to decide how their identity information is used.

Transparency in identity governance is essential for maintaining trust between organizations and users. Many identity management solutions operate behind the scenes, making decisions about authentication, access rights, and identity verification without user awareness. Ethical IAM practices involve providing users with visibility into how their identity data is processed, stored, and shared. Organizations must clearly communicate data retention policies, authentication methods, and identity verification requirements to ensure that users understand how their digital identities are managed.

Minimization of identity data collection is another ethical consideration. Organizations often collect excessive user data beyond what is necessary for authentication or access control. This over-collection increases privacy risks and exposes users to potential data breaches. Ethical identity management follows the principle of data minimization, where only the least amount of personally identifiable information (PII) required for authentication is collected and retained. For example, biometric authentication should store only encrypted biometric templates rather than raw fingerprint or facial scan data.

Bias in identity verification and authentication systems presents a growing ethical challenge, particularly in biometric authentication, facial recognition, and AI-driven identity analytics. Studies have shown that some identity verification systems exhibit bias against individuals based on race, gender, age, or disability. Facial recognition algorithms, for instance, have been found to perform less accurately for people with darker skin tones or non-binary gender identities. Ethical identity management requires organizations to develop and test IAM systems using diverse datasets, ensuring that identity verification processes are inclusive, unbiased, and equitable for all users.

The ethical implications of identity tracking and surveillance raise concerns about privacy rights and government overreach. Many organizations and government agencies implement continuous identity monitoring, behavioral tracking, and geolocation-based authentication to enhance security. However, these practices can lead to excessive surveillance, where users are tracked without their knowledge or consent. Ethical IAM policies should define clear limitations on identity tracking, ensuring that monitoring practices respect user privacy while achieving necessary security objectives.

Organizations must implement data anonymization, encryption, and user notification mechanisms to reduce the risks of mass surveillance.

The right to be forgotten and identity data deletion is an ethical issue in digital identity management. Many users are unaware that their identity data remains stored in IAM systems long after they stop using a service. Ethical identity management policies should provide users with the ability to request data deletion, account deactivation, and identity record removal when they no longer wish to maintain a digital identity with an organization. Compliance with GDPR and similar regulations requires businesses to honor user requests for data erasure while ensuring that identity data is not retained longer than necessary.

Identity fraud and ethical responsibilities in protecting digital identities are crucial concerns for IAM providers and organizations handling sensitive user data. Identity theft, phishing attacks, and account takeovers result in financial and reputational damage for individuals. Ethical identity management involves proactively securing user identities through strong encryption, multi-factor authentication (MFA), and fraud detection mechanisms. Organizations must take responsibility for protecting users against identity-related cyber threats, rather than shifting the burden of security entirely onto individuals.

Decentralized identity and self-sovereign identity (SSI) introduce new ethical opportunities and challenges. Traditional IAM systems rely on centralized identity providers (IdPs) that control user authentication and access management. Decentralized identity solutions, based on blockchain and cryptographic trust models, allow users to control their own digital identities without reliance on third-party intermediaries. While decentralized identity enhances privacy and reduces the risk of centralized data breaches, it also raises ethical concerns regarding identity fraud, lack of regulatory oversight, and potential exclusion of users who lack access to digital identity technologies. Ethical IAM implementations should ensure that decentralized identity solutions are accessible, verifiable, and interoperable with existing authentication frameworks.

The ethical responsibilities of AI in identity management require careful oversight. AI-driven IAM solutions use machine learning algorithms to detect fraud, automate identity verification, and enforce access policies. However, AI systems can introduce false positives, biased decision-making, and lack of transparency in identity verification processes. Ethical identity management mandates that AI-based IAM systems remain explainable, auditable, and subject to human oversight. Organizations should implement AI ethics frameworks that address bias mitigation, user rights protections, and algorithmic fairness in identity security.

The ethical implications of biometric data usage must be carefully managed to prevent misuse and privacy violations. Biometric authentication methods, such as fingerprint scanning, facial recognition, and voice recognition, provide enhanced security but also raise concerns about data permanence, biometric spoofing, and government misuse. Unlike passwords, biometric data cannot be changed once compromised. Ethical IAM policies must ensure that biometric data is encrypted, stored securely, and used only with explicit user consent. Organizations should also provide alternative authentication methods for users who are uncomfortable sharing biometric data.

Digital identity and access equity is an emerging ethical challenge as more services transition to online platforms. Individuals in underserved communities, those with disabilities, or people without formal government-issued identification often face barriers to accessing digital services. Ethical IAM strategies must address these inequities by providing inclusive identity verification options, multilingual authentication interfaces, and support for individuals who lack traditional identity documents. Organizations should design IAM systems that promote accessibility, usability, and non-discriminatory identity verification practices.

Organizations managing digital identities have a responsibility to uphold ethical standards that prioritize privacy, fairness, transparency, and user empowerment. Ethical identity management is not just about compliance with regulations but about respecting user autonomy, preventing identity-related harm, and promoting trust in digital systems. By adopting responsible IAM policies, organizations can ensure that identity security aligns with ethical principles, providing a balanced approach between security and user rights in the evolving digital landscape.

Identity and Privacy Regulations Around the World

Identity and privacy regulations vary across jurisdictions, reflecting different legal frameworks, cultural perspectives, and governmental approaches to data protection. As digital identities become central to online interactions, organizations must navigate a complex landscape of global regulations to ensure compliance while managing identity securely. Many regulations focus on protecting personally identifiable information (PII), enforcing user consent, and establishing legal accountability for identity misuse. Understanding the global regulatory landscape is essential for businesses operating across borders, as failure to comply with identity and privacy laws can lead to financial penalties, legal action, and reputational damage.

One of the most influential identity and privacy regulations is the General Data Protection Regulation (GDPR), which applies to organizations operating in the European Union (EU) and those processing the data of EU residents. GDPR enforces strict requirements for data collection, processing, and storage, ensuring that individuals have greater control over their digital identities. Organizations must obtain explicit consent before processing personal data, and users have the right to access, modify, and delete their identity information. GDPR also mandates the implementation of strong encryption, data minimization practices, and breach notification policies. Companies found in violation of GDPR face heavy penalties, which can amount to up to 4% of their global annual revenue or €20 million, whichever is higher.

In the United States (US), privacy regulations are more fragmented, with sector-specific and state-level laws governing identity and data protection. The California Consumer Privacy Act (CCPA) provides California residents with rights similar to those under GDPR, including the ability to opt out of data sharing, request data deletion, and access personal information collected by businesses. The California Privacy Rights Act (CPRA) strengthens CCPA by introducing new consumer rights, stricter data protection obligations, and enforcement mechanisms. Beyond California, other states such as Virginia, Colorado, and Utah have enacted their own privacy laws, contributing to a growing patchwork of identity regulations across the US.

In Canada, identity and privacy protection is governed by the Personal Information Protection and Electronic Documents Act (PIPEDA). This federal law establishes guidelines for the collection, use, and disclosure of personal information by private-sector organizations. PIPEDA emphasizes informed consent, transparency, and accountability, requiring organizations to protect digital identities through secure authentication, access controls, and encryption. Additionally, some Canadian provinces, such as British Columbia and Quebec, have enacted their own privacy laws that impose stricter identity protection requirements.

In Latin America, several countries have adopted GDPR-like frameworks to strengthen identity and data protection. Brazil's General Data Protection Law (LGPD) regulates how businesses collect and process personal data, emphasizing user rights, corporate accountability, and data security. LGPD applies to companies handling Brazilian citizens' identity data, regardless of where the company is based. Similarly, Argentina's Personal Data Protection Law enforces strict rules on digital identity management, requiring organizations to obtain explicit consent for data processing and implement secure access controls.

In Asia-Pacific, identity and privacy regulations vary significantly across different nations. China's Personal Information Protection Law (PIPL) is one of the most comprehensive data protection laws in the region, governing how businesses collect, store, and transfer Chinese citizens' identity data. PIPL imposes strict cross-border data transfer restrictions, requiring businesses to store sensitive identity data within China unless specific exemptions apply. The law also mandates risk assessments for identity processing activities and introduces harsh penalties for non-compliance. In Japan, the Act on the Protection of Personal Information (APPI) regulates digital identity management, ensuring that individuals have the right to access, correct, and request the deletion of their personal data. Japan has also aligned APPI with GDPR standards to facilitate international data transfers.

India's Digital Personal Data Protection Act (DPDPA) introduces a regulatory framework for identity and privacy protection, requiring organizations to implement data minimization, user consent mechanisms, and security safeguards. The law grants Indian citizens greater control over their digital identities, allowing them to request data correction, access, and deletion. The Indian government also enforces strict regulations on biometric identity management, particularly in relation to Aadhaar, the country's national digital identity system.

In Australia, the Privacy Act 1988 and the Australian Privacy Principles (APPs) govern identity and data protection. Organizations must ensure that personal data is collected lawfully, stored securely, and used only for intended purposes. The Australian government has also introduced Consumer Data Rights (CDR), allowing individuals to control how their identity information is shared with financial institutions, telecommunications providers, and energy companies.

The Middle East and Africa are also strengthening their identity and privacy regulations. The United Arab Emirates (UAE) Personal Data Protection Law and Saudi Arabia's Personal Data Protection Law (PDPL) establish frameworks for secure identity management, consent-based data processing, and cross-border data transfer restrictions. In South Africa, the Protection of Personal Information Act (POPIA) enforces strict data security measures, ensuring that digital identities are protected against unauthorized access and identity fraud.

Organizations operating in multiple jurisdictions must adopt privacy-by-design principles to comply with global identity regulations. This involves integrating strong authentication mechanisms, data encryption, identity access controls, and compliance reporting tools into identity management systems. Companies also implement privacy-enhancing technologies (PETs), such as anonymization, pseudonymization, and decentralized identity models, to minimize regulatory risks while ensuring secure identity verification.

Cross-border identity data transfers remain a significant challenge in global compliance. Many regulations impose data localization requirements, preventing businesses from storing or processing identity information outside their national boundaries. Companies use frameworks such as Standard Contractual Clauses (SCCs), Binding Corporate Rules (BCRs), and international data transfer agreements to ensure that identity data is handled legally when crossing international borders.

Identity and privacy regulations continue to evolve as governments respond to emerging security threats, technological advancements, and public concerns about digital identity misuse. Organizations must stay informed about regulatory updates, compliance requirements, and industry best practices to navigate the complex global identity management landscape effectively. By integrating secure authentication, ethical data processing, and robust access controls, businesses can ensure compliance while maintaining user trust in the digital world.

Case Studies in Successful Identity Lifecycle Implementations

Organizations across industries have recognized the importance of identity lifecycle management (ILM) in securing access to digital assets, streamlining user provisioning, and ensuring compliance with regulatory frameworks. Successful implementations of ILM demonstrate how automation, integration with human resources (HR) systems, and risk-based access controls contribute to improved security and operational efficiency. The following case studies highlight real-world implementations of ILM that have significantly enhanced identity governance and access management.

A leading global financial institution faced challenges in managing identities across its complex, multi-cloud environment. The company operated in multiple regions, requiring seamless authentication and access control for employees, contractors, and third-party vendors. Before implementing an ILM solution, identity provisioning and deprovisioning were handled manually, leading to delays in access approvals, orphaned accounts, and compliance risks. The financial institution adopted an AI-driven identity governance platform that integrated with HR systems, enabling automated role-based provisioning based on job function, location, and department. When an employee was onboarded, the system automatically assigned access to required applications based on predefined policies. If an employee changed roles or left the company, access was adjusted or revoked instantly. The implementation reduced onboarding time by 60%, eliminated orphaned accounts, and ensured compliance with SOX and GDPR regulations.

A large healthcare provider with thousands of employees, clinicians, and support staff struggled with manual access management processes, which resulted in security gaps and inefficiencies. The healthcare organization needed a way to enforce least privilege access while ensuring that medical professionals had timely access to patient records and clinical systems. The implementation of a role-based access control (RBAC) model integrated with the hospital's electronic health record (EHR) system helped streamline access provisioning. Each employee was assigned access based on their role (e.g., doctor, nurse, administrator), ensuring that only authorized personnel could access sensitive medical data. The ILM system also enforced multi-factor authentication (MFA) for privileged users, reducing the risk of credential theft. As a result, the healthcare provider saw a 40% reduction in unauthorized access incidents and improved compliance with HIPAA regulations.

A multinational technology company faced challenges in managing privileged access for IT administrators and DevOps teams. The company had multiple data centers, cloud environments, and software development teams that required temporary elevated access for system configurations and debugging. Before implementing an ILM solution, administrators had persistent access to high-risk systems, increasing the risk of insider threats and credential abuse. The company adopted a just-in-time (JIT) privileged access management (PAM) solution, which granted temporary administrative access based on contextual risk factors. When an IT engineer needed access to a production environment, the system evaluated the request, verified the risk level, and granted access for a limited time. If unusual behavior was detected, such as an administrator logging in from an unrecognized device, the system automatically revoked access and triggered an alert. The implementation resulted in a 75% reduction in privileged access misuse incidents and improved compliance with ISO 27001 security standards.

A government agency responsible for citizen services struggled with identity verification challenges due to an outdated manual process for onboarding new users. The agency needed a scalable ILM solution to authenticate citizens securely while preventing identity fraud. The implementation of a biometric identity verification system combined with AI-driven fraud detection transformed the agency's identity lifecycle management. When citizens registered for government services, they were required to verify their identity using facial recognition and document authentication. AI algorithms cross-referenced user-provided identity data with government databases to detect potential fraud. The system also supported federated authentication, allowing citizens to use their verified identity across multiple government services. As a result, the agency saw an 80% reduction in fraudulent identity registrations, improved citizen service efficiency, and increased trust in government digital services.

A global e-commerce company needed to improve its customer identity and access management (CIAM) while enhancing security and user experience. Before implementing an ILM solution, customers faced frequent authentication friction, leading to abandoned transactions and poor engagement. The company introduced a risk-based authentication framework that dynamically adjusted security requirements based on user behavior. Customers logging in from recognized devices were granted seamless access, while those exhibiting unusual login patterns (e.g., accessing from a high-risk region) were required to complete additional verification steps. The ILM system also integrated passwordless authentication, allowing customers to sign in using biometric recognition or security tokens instead of traditional passwords. The implementation led to a 30% increase in customer retention, a 50% reduction in account takeover fraud, and improved compliance with PCI-DSS security requirements.

A large manufacturing enterprise needed an ILM solution to manage the identity lifecycle of IoT devices and machine identities. The company operated automated production lines, industrial sensors, and robotics, requiring strong identity governance for non-human entities. The implementation of an IoT identity management platform enabled secure device onboarding, certificate-based authentication, and real-time identity monitoring. Each device was assigned a unique cryptographic identity, ensuring that only authorized machines could communicate within the network. AI-driven monitoring detected anomalous device behavior, triggering automated security responses if a compromised IoT device attempted unauthorized access. The implementation improved supply chain security, reduced IoT-related cyber threats by 65%, and enhanced compliance with NIST IoT security guidelines.

A global investment firm needed to modernize its identity lifecycle processes for a hybrid workforce that included full-time employees, contractors, and external consultants. The firm adopted an identity orchestration platform that automated user provisioning, access certifications, and compliance reporting. The system integrated with cloud IAM solutions, HR systems, and third-party authentication providers, ensuring that user identities were managed consistently across on-premises and cloud environments. The implementation of self-service access request workflows reduced IT support ticket volumes by 50%, while automated access reviews ensured compliance with financial industry regulations such as SOX and Basel II. The firm also leveraged AI-driven identity analytics to detect unusual access patterns, reducing security incidents related to insider threats by 45%.

Successful identity lifecycle implementations demonstrate how automation, AI, and strong governance frameworks improve security, operational efficiency, and compliance. By leveraging automated identity provisioning, adaptive authentication, privileged access management, and IoT identity security, organizations across industries have strengthened their IAM strategies while enhancing user experience and risk management. These case studies highlight the transformative impact of well-designed identity lifecycle management systems, setting benchmarks for future IAM advancements.

Common Pitfalls and How to Avoid Them

Implementing identity lifecycle management (ILM) presents numerous challenges that, if not properly addressed, can lead to security vulnerabilities, compliance failures, and operational inefficiencies. Many organizations struggle with misconfigurations, poor governance, and inadequate automation, which can expose user accounts to unauthorized access and increase the risk of identity-related breaches. By understanding common pitfalls in ILM and implementing proactive strategies, organizations can enhance security, streamline identity workflows, and maintain compliance with regulatory requirements.

One of the most frequent mistakes in ILM is failing to implement automated provisioning and deprovisioning. Many organizations still rely on manual identity management processes, which can lead to delays in granting or revoking access. Employees, contractors, and third-party vendors may retain access to critical systems long after their roles have changed or their contracts have ended, increasing the risk of orphaned accounts. To avoid this, organizations should integrate ILM solutions with HR systems, directory services, and cloud identity platforms to enable real-time user provisioning and deprovisioning. Automating identity workflows ensures that users receive appropriate access based on their job function and that their access is promptly revoked when no longer needed.

Another major pitfall is over-permissioning users and failing to enforce least privilege access. Many organizations assign broad permissions to users without properly assessing their actual access needs. This practice increases the risk of privilege creep, where users accumulate unnecessary access rights over time. Attackers who compromise an over-permissioned account can escalate privileges, access sensitive data, and move laterally within the network. Implementing role-based access control (RBAC) and attribute-based access control (ABAC) helps enforce the principle of least privilege by ensuring that users only have access to the resources they need to perform their job functions. Periodic access reviews and certification processes should also be conducted to identify and remove excessive permissions.

Neglecting privileged access management (PAM) is another common mistake in ILM. Administrative and high-privilege accounts require stricter security controls because they provide access to critical systems and sensitive data. Organizations that fail to secure privileged accounts risk credential theft, insider threats, and privilege escalation attacks. To mitigate this risk, businesses should implement just-in-time (JIT) access provisioning, which grants privileged access only for a limited time and based on specific approval workflows. Additionally, privileged session monitoring, audit logging, and multi-factor authentication (MFA) enforcement should be applied to all administrative accounts to prevent unauthorized access.

Ignoring identity governance and compliance requirements can lead to regulatory violations and security gaps. Many industries are subject to strict compliance frameworks such as GDPR, HIPAA, PCI-DSS, and SOX, which mandate strong identity access controls and audit mechanisms. Organizations that lack proper identity governance may struggle with access audits, user certification reviews, and security reporting, increasing their risk of non-compliance penalties. Implementing an identity governance framework with automated compliance reporting, policy enforcement, and access recertification workflows helps organizations maintain regulatory adherence while ensuring identity security.

Poor password management and weak authentication policies create significant security vulnerabilities. Many organizations still rely on password-based authentication without implementing multi-factor authentication (MFA) or passwordless authentication methods. Weak or reused passwords are one of the leading causes of identity breaches, as they can be easily compromised through phishing attacks, credential stuffing, and brute force attempts. Organizations should enforce strong password policies, encourage the use of password managers, and adopt modern authentication methods such as FIDO2-based security keys and biometric authentication to strengthen identity security.

Another common pitfall is failing to manage non-human identities properly. Many organizations focus only on human users while neglecting machine identities, API credentials, and IoT devices that require authentication and authorization. Cybercriminals often exploit weakly secured service accounts, hardcoded credentials, and exposed API keys to gain unauthorized access to systems. Organizations should implement certificate-based authentication, automated credential rotation, and machine identity governance to secure non-human identities and prevent unauthorized access to critical systems.

Lack of visibility into identity-related activities hinders security monitoring and incident response. Organizations that do not actively monitor authentication logs, access patterns, and privileged account activity may miss early indicators of identity-related threats. Attackers often attempt to exploit identity weaknesses through suspicious login attempts, unusual access requests, and privilege escalation activities. To enhance visibility, organizations should deploy security information and event management (SIEM) solutions, user and entity behavior analytics (UEBA), and AI-driven identity threat detection tools. Continuous identity monitoring allows security teams to detect and respond to potential identity threats before they escalate into full-scale breaches.

Poor integration between identity systems and business applications creates inefficiencies and security gaps. Many organizations use fragmented identity solutions that do not communicate with each other, leading to manual workarounds, inconsistent access controls, and increased security risks. To avoid these challenges, businesses should adopt identity orchestration platforms that centralize authentication, access control, and identity governance across on-premises, cloud, and hybrid environments. Integrating IAM solutions with single sign-on (SSO), federation protocols (SAML, OpenID Connect), and identity-as-a-service (IDaaS) providers ensures seamless identity management across multiple platforms.

Another major issue is not implementing adaptive and risk-based authentication. Many organizations apply static authentication policies that do not consider contextual risk factors. This approach leaves systems vulnerable to compromised credentials, as attackers can exploit stolen passwords to gain access without triggering security alerts. Implementing risk-based authentication (RBA) ensures that access decisions are dynamically adjusted based on login behavior, device reputation, geographic location, and past authentication history. High-risk login attempts should trigger additional authentication challenges, while low-risk users should be granted frictionless access.

Finally, ignoring identity lifecycle management for departing employees and contractors poses significant security risks. Organizations that do not promptly deactivate user accounts when employees leave may inadvertently allow former employees to retain access to corporate systems. This creates opportunities for data exfiltration, insider threats, and unauthorized access to sensitive resources. Automating deprovisioning workflows, revoking access upon termination, and regularly auditing inactive accounts ensures that user identities are properly managed throughout their lifecycle.

Avoiding common pitfalls in identity lifecycle management requires a proactive approach that integrates automation, strong access controls, continuous monitoring, and compliance enforcement. By implementing best practices, organizations can enhance security, reduce identity-related risks, and improve overall operational efficiency in their IAM programs.

Roadmap to a Mature Identity Lifecycle Strategy

A mature identity lifecycle strategy is essential for organizations to effectively manage digital identities, enforce security policies, and maintain compliance with regulatory frameworks. As enterprises scale and adopt cloud-based services, hybrid IT environments, and remote work models, managing user and machine identities becomes increasingly complex. A well-structured identity lifecycle strategy ensures that identities are created, assigned appropriate access, monitored for risks, and deprovisioned when no longer needed. Organizations must take a structured approach to achieving maturity in identity lifecycle management (ILM), balancing automation, security, and governance to reduce identity-related risks.

The foundation of a mature identity lifecycle strategy begins with establishing a centralized identity governance framework. Many organizations operate in fragmented environments where identity management is handled separately across on-premises directories, cloud services, and third-party applications. This siloed approach creates inefficiencies, security gaps, and compliance risks. A centralized identity governance model integrates all identity data into a unified system, ensuring consistent policies and access controls across the enterprise. Organizations should leverage identity and access management (IAM) solutions that support hybrid environments, integrating with on-premises Active Directory (AD), cloud identity providers like Azure AD, and federated identity platforms.

Automating user provisioning and deprovisioning is a critical step toward identity lifecycle maturity. Manual identity management processes introduce delays, human errors, and security vulnerabilities such as orphaned accounts. Organizations must integrate ILM with human resources (HR) systems to enable real-time provisioning based on employment status changes. When a new employee is onboarded, access should be granted automatically based on their role, department, and location. Similarly, when an employee leaves the company, all access should be revoked instantly to prevent unauthorized access. Automating these workflows reduces IT workload, enhances security, and ensures compliance with data protection regulations.

A mature identity lifecycle strategy also requires implementing role-based and attribute-based access controls (RBAC and ABAC). Traditional access models often lead to over-permissioned users, increasing the risk of privilege creep and insider threats. RBAC assigns users access based on predefined job roles, ensuring that employees only have the permissions necessary for their function. ABAC enhances this model by incorporating contextual attributes, such as device type, geographic location, and security clearance, to make dynamic access decisions. By implementing RBAC and ABAC, organizations enforce least privilege access, reducing the attack surface and improving security posture.

Adopting risk-based authentication and adaptive access controls is another key component of a mature identity lifecycle strategy. Traditional authentication models apply static security policies, treating all login attempts equally regardless of risk factors. This outdated approach makes systems vulnerable to credential theft and phishing attacks. Implementing risk-based authentication (RBA) enhances security by dynamically adjusting authentication requirements based on real-time risk analysis. Factors such as login behavior, device reputation, and geographic anomalies help determine whether a user should be granted access, required to provide additional verification (multi-factor authentication), or blocked entirely. This approach strengthens security without introducing unnecessary friction for legitimate users.

Managing privileged identities and administrative accounts is essential for preventing unauthorized access to critical systems. Privileged accounts, such as IT administrators and cloud service managers, require enhanced security controls due to their elevated access. Organizations should implement just-in-time (JIT) privileged access management (PAM), granting temporary administrative privileges only when needed. Instead of maintaining always-on privileged accounts, JIT-PAM enforces time-limited access, reducing the risk of credential theft and privilege abuse. Additionally, privileged access should be monitored using session recording, audit logging, and AI-driven anomaly detection to detect and respond to suspicious activity.

A mature identity lifecycle strategy also incorporates continuous identity monitoring and anomaly detection. Identity-related threats often go unnoticed in organizations that lack real-time visibility into authentication events, access patterns, and privilege escalations. Deploying user and entity behavior analytics (UEBA) allows organizations to detect deviations from normal behavior, failed authentication attempts, and unauthorized access attempts. AI-powered IAM solutions enhance security by identifying compromised credentials, insider threats, and high-risk user activities, enabling automated incident response.

Enhancing identity security for non-human identities is an emerging challenge that organizations must address in their identity lifecycle strategy. Many businesses focus on managing human user identities while neglecting machine identities, API credentials, and IoT devices that require authentication. Cybercriminals exploit poorly managed machine identities to launch attacks on enterprise networks. Implementing certificate-based authentication, API key rotation, and machine identity governance ensures that non-human entities are properly secured and cannot be exploited by attackers.

Ensuring compliance with global identity regulations is a critical milestone in achieving identity lifecycle maturity. Organizations must comply with laws such as GDPR, HIPAA, CCPA, PCI-DSS, and NIST 800-63, which mandate identity verification, data encryption, access controls, and audit reporting. Mature ILM strategies integrate automated compliance reporting, access certification campaigns, and policy enforcement mechanisms to ensure that identity security meets regulatory standards. Implementing a zero trust architecture, which requires continuous identity validation and strict access segmentation, further strengthens compliance efforts.

Identity lifecycle maturity also requires self-service identity management capabilities that empower users while reducing administrative burdens on IT teams. Self-service IAM portals enable employees and customers to reset passwords, request access, update authentication settings, and manage their own identity attributes without requiring IT intervention. Organizations should implement AI-powered chatbots and virtual assistants to streamline identity-related requests, improving both user experience and security.

A forward-thinking identity lifecycle strategy must incorporate decentralized identity and self-sovereign identity (SSI) models. Traditional identity systems rely on centralized identity providers, which create single points of failure and privacy risks. Decentralized identity allows users to control their own digital identities using blockchain-based verifiable credentials and decentralized identifiers (DIDs). While still in the early stages of adoption, decentralized identity enhances privacy, security, and cross-platform authentication, making it a key consideration for future IAM strategies.

Finally, organizations must implement identity lifecycle resilience and incident response planning to address identity-related security breaches. Despite best practices, identity theft, credential leaks, and unauthorized access incidents will occur. Organizations should establish identity breach detection frameworks, automated incident response workflows, and forensic investigation capabilities to quickly contain and mitigate identity threats. Implementing identity risk scoring, AI-driven breach detection, and dark web monitoring ensures that organizations can proactively identify and respond to identity-related security risks.

A mature identity lifecycle strategy is continuous and adaptive, evolving with technological advancements, regulatory changes, and emerging cybersecurity threats. Organizations that invest in identity automation, risk-based authentication, identity governance, and AI-driven security analytics build a strong foundation for managing digital identities securely and efficiently. By following a structured roadmap toward identity lifecycle maturity, businesses enhance security, compliance, and user trust while reducing operational complexities in IAM management.

Conclusion and Next Steps in Identity Lifecycle Management

Identity lifecycle management (ILM) has become a critical component of modern cybersecurity and business operations. Organizations of all sizes must manage user identities effectively, ensuring that individuals and systems have the appropriate level of access at all times while preventing unauthorized access. A well-implemented ILM strategy enables businesses to enhance security, improve efficiency, and comply with regulatory requirements. As identity-related threats continue to evolve, organizations must take a proactive approach to refining and strengthening their ILM programs.

The foundation of a strong ILM strategy lies in automation and integration. Many organizations still rely on manual processes for provisioning and deprovisioning accounts, which leads to inefficiencies, security gaps, and compliance risks. Integrating ILM with human resources (HR) systems ensures that new employees receive immediate access to necessary resources while automatically revoking access when they leave the company. Automated role-based access control (RBAC) and attribute-based access control (ABAC) further streamline access management by ensuring that users are only granted permissions that align with their job functions. The adoption of identity orchestration platforms and cloud-based identity-as-a-service (IDaaS) solutions can help organizations centralize and automate identity management across on-premises and cloud environments.

Multi-factor authentication (MFA) and risk-based access controls have become essential in mitigating identity-related security risks. Traditional password-based authentication is no longer sufficient, as stolen credentials remain a leading cause of data breaches. Implementing MFA ensures that even if credentials are compromised, attackers cannot easily gain access to systems. Organizations should also adopt risk-based authentication (RBA), which dynamically adjusts security measures based on user behavior, device reputation, and geographic location. Adaptive security mechanisms prevent unauthorized access without creating unnecessary friction for legitimate users.

Privileged access management (PAM) is another crucial area that organizations must continue to refine. Privileged accounts, such as IT administrators and system operators, pose a high-security risk if not managed properly. Cybercriminals often target these accounts to gain elevated access to critical systems. Implementing just-in-time (JIT) access, session monitoring, and credential vaulting can significantly reduce the risk of privilege abuse. Organizations should also enforce continuous monitoring and behavioral analytics to detect suspicious privileged account activity in real time.

The rise of decentralized identity and self-sovereign identity (SSI) presents an opportunity for organizations to rethink traditional identity models. Rather than relying on centralized identity providers, decentralized identity solutions leverage blockchain and cryptographic verification to enable users to control their own digital identities. This approach enhances privacy, reduces the risk of identity theft, and minimizes reliance on single points of failure. While decentralized identity is still in the early stages of adoption, organizations should explore how it can be integrated into existing IAM frameworks for enhanced security and user empowerment.

Compliance with global identity regulations is an ongoing challenge that organizations must address. Governments worldwide are enacting stricter data protection laws, such as GDPR in Europe, CCPA in California, LGPD in Brazil, and PIPL in China, which impose stringent requirements on identity governance. Organizations must continuously assess their ILM policies to ensure compliance with evolving legal standards. Implementing automated compliance reporting, access certification workflows, and real-time audit logging helps businesses demonstrate adherence to regulatory frameworks while reducing administrative overhead.

Artificial intelligence (AI) and machine learning (ML) are transforming ILM by enabling predictive analytics, anomaly detection, and intelligent automation. AI-driven identity threat detection systems analyze user behavior patterns to identify deviations that may indicate compromised accounts or insider threats. Machine learning algorithms help refine access control decisions, detect privilege escalation attempts, and automate identity risk assessments. By leveraging AI-powered identity governance solutions, organizations can stay ahead of emerging security threats while improving operational efficiency.

Another important next step in ILM is the adoption of Zero Trust security models. Traditional perimeter-based security approaches are no longer effective in an era where employees work remotely, cloud applications are widespread, and cyber threats are increasingly sophisticated. Zero Trust enforces the principle of "never trust, always verify", requiring continuous authentication and strict access controls for every user and device. Organizations implementing Zero Trust must integrate continuous identity verification, micro-segmentation, and real-time risk-based authentication to prevent unauthorized access and lateral movement within networks.

Organizations must also focus on securing machine identities, as non-human entities such as IoT devices, cloud services, and APIs require authentication just like human users. Many businesses fail to manage these identities properly, leading to security vulnerabilities. Implementing certificate-based authentication, automated key rotation, and API security controls ensures that machine identities remain secure throughout their lifecycle. Identity governance frameworks should include policies for monitoring and auditing service accounts, IoT device authentication, and third-party integrations.

Enhancing user experience while maintaining security is a key consideration for future ILM improvements. Frictionless authentication methods, such as passwordless authentication using biometrics, security keys, and push notifications, improve user convenience while reducing reliance on weak passwords. Implementing self-service IAM portals empowers users to manage their own access requests, password resets, and identity verification without requiring IT support. Organizations should also explore identity federation and single sign-on (SSO) solutions to streamline authentication across multiple applications and platforms.

A well-defined incident response plan for identity-related breaches is an essential component of a mature ILM strategy. Despite best practices, identity compromises can still occur, making it crucial for organizations to have real-time monitoring, automated incident response, and forensic investigation capabilities in place. Deploying SIEM (Security Information and Event Management) systems, automated breach detection tools, and identity threat intelligence platforms ensures that organizations can quickly detect and contain identity-related security incidents before they escalate.

Looking ahead, organizations must remain adaptable to emerging identity security trends and technological advancements. Cyber threats are constantly evolving, and identity lifecycle management must evolve with them. Businesses that invest in AI-driven automation, continuous identity verification, and Zero Trust security will be better positioned to defend against identity-based attacks and regulatory challenges.

A successful identity lifecycle strategy requires ongoing evaluation, continuous improvement, and alignment with business objectives. Organizations should regularly assess their ILM maturity, conduct security audits, and optimize access controls based on real-world threat intelligence. By fostering a culture of security awareness, identity governance, and proactive risk management, businesses can protect their digital identities, enhance compliance, and create a seamless user experience.

Identity lifecycle management is not just about security—it is about enabling trust, innovation, and resilience in an increasingly digital world. Organizations that prioritize automation, intelligent authentication, and identity governance will be well-equipped to navigate the complexities of modern identity management while maintaining a competitive edge in their industry.